The Making of
The Jewel in the Crown

The Making of
The
Jewel

**The Masterpiece Theatre series
based on Paul Scott's *Raj Quartet***

in the
Crown

St. Martin's Press • New York

Stills photography by Stewart Darby and David Burrows

Library of Congress Cataloging in Publication Data
Main entry under title:

The Making of The jewel in the crown.

   Based on Paul Scott's The Raj quartet.
   1. Jewel in the crown (Television program)
2. India—History—Drama.   I. Scott, Paul, 1920-1978
Raj quartet.
PN1992.77.J38M35   1984   791.45'72   84-11762
ISBN 0-312-50705-4 (pbk.)

Contents

The Making of
The Jewel in the Crown

❧ I ❧

Introduction

by Sir Denis Forman, Chairman of Granada Television

The sun rose on Paul Scott's literary reputation when *Staying On* won the Booker Prize in 1977. Along with thousands of others I read it with delight, and recognized that here was a natural for television. *Staying On* led me to the 'Raj Quartet', and immediately I was back in the India that I had known in the years before Independence. As I made my way through the labyrinthine narrative, it became clear that the Quartet was an epic story on the scale of *War and Peace*, introducing a galère of characters every bit as real as those in Tolstoy's novel, and like them playing out their parts within a greater plot concerned with national politics and a world war.

On second reading I wondered if the Quartet might be susceptible to television. The rights were free. It could be the chance of a lifetime.

Could it be done on television? The narrative was told in a form so complex as to make all the flash-backery of Conrad and Ford Madox Ford look like a children's game. The book was heavy with references to a political scene that was never familiar and today almost wholly forgotten by the Western world. At least four months shooting in India would be needed, and no unit from the United Kingdom or America had at that time attempted anything on such a scale (Richard Attenborough's *Gandhi* was not shot until 1981).

It seemed sensible, indeed necessary, to do two things before committing Granada to such a major operation. First, we would make *Staying On* in Simla as a single play and so gain some experience to help us decide whether the logistics and cost of a lengthy shoot in a distant sub-continent were within our reach. Also, before recruiting a production team, we must be satisfied that it was possible to do justice to the Quartet if it were translated into the form of a television series.

Staying On was made in 1980. Although there were problems in plenty, the finished film, with Trevor Howard and Celia Johnson as Tusker and Lucy, was much liked. Meanwhile, I had set about an exercise on the Quartet. The first step was to arrange all the events in the story into chronological order, starting from the riots of 1942 and continuing until Guy Perron flew towards Delhi in the week of Independence in July 1947. It was not a simple task. Some incidents were told and retold a second and third time. There were no less than thirteen separate references to the rape, each one throwing some new emphasis or a different interpretation upon it. There were excursions off the main track (notably the opening tragic story of Miss Crane). There were a great number of direct references to the political scene. There were seven main geographical locations, and, worst of all, we lost our first hero and heroine, Hari Kumar and Daphne Manners, just as they had aroused our interest and engaged our sympathy.

The next move was to see how the chronological narrative would break down into sequences each of which would form a one hour episode for the television screen. This was done by chopping a roll of wallpaper into thirteen segments about one yard square, pinning them round the walls of a room and writing down on each the outline of scenes for each episode. After walking some miles around this gallery, touching, retouching, shifting and deliberating, it did, at last, seem feasible that Paul Scott's great book could be made into a television series that would not betray the quality of the original work. Meanwhile, Irene Shubik, the producer of *Staying On*, who had long been pondering the same problem, had reached her own conclusions. She had never doubted it could be done: we shared our findings and she took over the reins and invited Ken Taylor to write the early scripts. Although there were other scriptwriters in view, it soon became clear that the choice of Ken was the right one, and in the fullness of time (after Irene Shubik had left Granada) it fell to his lot to write all the episodes, now fourteen, for the series.

The scripts were the foundation upon which the Quartet had to stand, and it soon became clear that Ken had laid down a slab of concrete that was to survive all the stresses and strains of production and indeed the final realization of *The Jewel in the Crown* deviates surprisingly little from the original draft.

In 1980, Christopher Morahan decided to leave the National Theatre in order to devote three years of his life to the production of *The Jewel in the Crown*. With his strong feeling for the novels and his depth of experience in theatre and television, he brought to the production a rare combination of qualities. He was able both to direct seven of the fourteen episodes and at the same time to exercise control over a large number of people and great sums of money, for he is one of those unusual people equally suited to command an army corps in action or to direct actors in the most intimate scenes. Christopher's influence over the production has been all pervasive. It was he who recommended Jim O'Brien as the complementary director, and it was he who set out to build the production team, mainly from Granada's staff, and to assemble the truly splendid cast.

Here again, Paul Scott was our greatest ally; actors were eager to play some of the parts which they felt had belonged to them since they first read the novels. In particular, the performances of Tim Pigott-Smith as Merrick, and Peggy Ashcroft as Barbie had begun to form in their minds long before they knew that Granada was going to make the series.

And so early in 1981 Christopher launched into his year of planning and reconnaissance. After three trips to India, exploring dozens of locations, and after hundreds of interviews, 'Jewel' began to come alive as the planning process worked like yeast throughout the body of Granada in Manchester, subsequently spreading to London, Delhi and Bombay.

On 3 January 1982, I bade the production team farewell; many had never left the UK before, some had not gone much further than London or Blackpool. Their arms were swollen with strange serums, their skins were white, they were a little apprehensive – and so was I. Three months later I saw them again in Mysore, brown as berries, working from sunrise to sunset in a temperature of nearly 100° Fahrenheit. None were allergic to India and nearly all of them were in love with it. It was a rewarding moment and in a way the crowning experience of nearly thirty years of working on Granada productions, for they were a truly wonderful unit. The Indian spirit managed to survive wet Wales, a Lancashire winter, and the running-in of a huge warehouse on the banks of the Irwell as a film studio, its subsequent demolition by fire, the agony of rapid replanning to keep to the schedule, and the final mysteries of the finishing process which took some nine months.

At the time of writing this piece the real test of our enterprise lies ahead. How truly will we have conveyed Paul Scott's original to the world? Will Hari Kumar, Ronald Merrick, Sarah Layton and Count Bronowsky become for viewers the real people that we know them to be, for we have been their constant companions over the last three years? Is our way of telling history good enough? Will we succeed in conveying Scott's uncanny insight into the psychology of the two principals in this great confrontation, the British and India?

The main hope, I think, of all who have worked on it, is that the series *The Jewel in the Crown* will do justice so far as television can to Paul Scott's 'Raj Quartet'.

❧2❧

The Making of *The Jewel in the Crown*

by Bamber Gascoigne

On the first day of filming in India, before a foot of film had been exposed, an aged holy man turned up to bless the production. For the cast and crew, on that January morning in 1982, the weather at Udaipur seemed like an English summer's day, a delightful contrast to the exceptionally cold winter from which they had escaped only three days previously at Heathrow. They were enjoying themselves in shirt sleeves. But for the holy man this mild sun was the very depth of winter. Above his white cotton Gandhi-style dhoti he wore a battered tweed jacket.

He had brought with him an assistant and a portable shrine. Three of the production team and one member of the cast were chosen to take part in the ceremony. They were instructed to remove their shoes and to squat on the ground. The holy man, chanting all the while, marked each of their foreheads with sandalwood paste, tied a red and yellow woollen thread round their right wrists, and invited them to pelt his shrine with flowers. For his climax he seemed determined to assault the camera with a coconut. At this point the producer, Christopher Morahan, prudently stepped in and insisted on fulfilling this task himself, tapping the lens gently with the whiskered shell.

With the honours done, the old man departed as mysteriously as he had arrived. Apparently no film in India's prolific movie industry ever begins without the benefit of this ceremony, and the Granada team had the impression that the old man had made this his speciality. Within Hinduism the fourth and final stage of a devout male life is when a man becomes a *sannyasi*, leaving his home and family and wandering around without possessions, dependent entirely on small acts of charity. So perhaps this particular *sannyasi* had found an unusually glamorous way of spending these years of self-denial, and the Indian film industry – as thriving as our own between the wars – can be guaranteed to keep him busy. Normally he would be blessing a lavishly romantic production of some three or four hours, the amount of time it takes, with a great deal of singing and dancing, for an Indian hero and heroine to overcome the obstacles posed by caste or poverty or in-laws and to achieve matrimony. Without realizing it the old man had launched, that January in Udaipur, his most ambitious project – a fourteen-hour television saga of the love-hate relationship between Britain and India or, in terms of the traditional family themes of Indian films, a study of the final years of a forced marriage between the two countries followed by the agonies of divorce. And events were to prove that he had done his work well. Nearly four months later, when filming in India was finished on schedule in spite of appalling difficulties of illness, weather and bureaucracy, the verdict of one of the company was that the entire project had been 'dogged by good luck'. The coconut had not been there for nothing.

There had already been a foretaste of Indian problems and of the need for good luck, for it was something of a miracle that filming was able to begin on this scheduled Day One. Granada had allowed a generous three weeks for the gear to make its way through customs in Delhi, but it had been a close-run thing. Every day during those three weeks Bill Shephard, one of the Production Managers, had argued with customs officers while, outside, nine empty lorries stood by in readiness to convey the equipment to Udaipur. The disputed gear consisted of 300 containers, ranging in size from a three-ton generator to a suitcase full of aerosol sprays. In the weeks before departure Bill had bullied each department in Manchester – Scenery, Costume, Make-up, Lights, Secretarial, First-Aid – to crate up their equipment and to fill it in, item by tiny item, on the forms provided by Indian customs. The problem arose because three containers had been itemized on forms for Consumables whereas their contents were Non-Consumable – the distinction is crucial to customs officers all over the world, for everything which will not be consumed within the country must be re-exported or pay duty. At one time it was solemnly proposed that the best solution might be to fly all 300 crates back to Manchester and there to fill out the forms correctly. In the end a massive refundable indemnity was agreed upon, and the equipment was released just in time for the drive to Udaipur.

Meanwhile the other Production Manager, Ian Scaife, had been having a similar struggle in Bombay, where he had been trying to clear three large trucks which had arrived by sea. These were the vehicles of Location Caterers, a London-based mobile kitchen. Granada, accustomed only to television standards of catering on location, had been intending to send to India the traditional 'butty-wagon', a vehicle capable of providing soups, salads, sandwiches and hot drinks in profusion but not much else. A contact on the production team for Sir Richard Attenborough's *Gandhi* had advised that this would be a psychological disaster among the trials of India, and had recommended the three cheerful Londoners, Tom, Roger and Frank, who had provided the midday needs of the *Gandhi* cast and crew. It was their vehicles which were now trapped in Bombay, again with everything separately listed on the innumerable forms, from awnings and folding tables and chairs down to individual knives and forks and paper plates and jars of Branston's pickle. The only objects which had been accidentally omitted from this list were so large that it is astonishing they passed unnoticed. They were six portable lavatories, stowed at the very farthest end of one lorry beyond the tomato ketchup. (Their eventual arrival on location, installed in a two-door Indian bus, was greeted with heartfelt applause.) In Bombay no fault was found with the forms, but there was the same incomprehensible delay. Both Bill and Ian swear that it was not a question of money changing hands, merely a fear on the part of the customs officers – invariably impeccable and charming in their behaviour – that they might accidentally put a foot wrong and so jeopardize their jobs. This may be so. But recognizing the occasion for generosity is a subtle matter, requiring long experience, and for the most part we travel in the East unaware of our opportunities.

Udaipur can make a strong claim to be the most beautiful city in India. In addition to the princely appeal of the palaces around and within its lake, its streets offer the everyday visual delights of India more pleasantly than anywhere else I know. They are too narrow to accommodate the usual throng of lorries and motorized rickshaws, and yet the shops and the painted houses are prosperous enough to look neat and calm. There is nothing fly-blown about this place. To anyone familiar with the less favoured parts of India, Udaipur looks even on an ordinary day as though it has been spruced up for a film. Yet it remains entirely real. For almost everyone working on *The Jewel in the Crown* this enchanting place

Preparing to embark for the short trip to the Lake Palace at Udaipur.

was their first experience of India – Delhi having been little more than an international airport and an international hotel – and for most it was the beginning of an exceptionally warm feeling of affection for the country and its people.

At this stage only one of the leading members of the cast knew something of India. Geraldine James, playing Sarah Layton, had also been in *Gandhi*. She was already an addict for all sights and sounds that were characteristically Indian, and on the first day in Delhi she had dragged some of her jet-lagged colleagues off to Chandni Chowk, the extremely crowded and bustling area of the city built three hundred years ago by Shah Jahan. They returned to the hotel somewhat shattered by the experience, but at Udaipur the assimilation of local colour was both more leisurely and more pleasant. Soon Geraldine and Tim Pigott-Smith (playing the central character of the series, Ronald Merrick) and some of the others were hiring bicycles to explore more fully the streets of the town – to the considerable alarm of the production team. But every tiny encounter helped to fill out the characterizations on which they would be working in the months ahead. Tim mentioned to me, as an example of an extremely shocking and helpful moment, the occasion when a jeep came dashing and honking its way through Udaipur, leaving the busy life of the street to scatter as best it might. It seemed to him exactly how Captain Merrick, the aggressive British police officer, would have driven through an Indian crowd, asserting at one and the same time his presence and his authority.

Ray Goode, Granada's Lighting Cameraman, had finished work on the thirteen-part series *Brideshead Revisited* only a few days before he was offered *The Jewel in the Crown*. Within a space of three years he would have completed nearly thirty hours

12

of film. For him Udaipur was the first chance to try out the giant portable reflectors which he had designed in England specifically to cope with the deep shadows cast by the Indian sun. Each could be unfolded to become a semi-rigid sheet, some twelve feet square, of silver balloon material. A pair of them would send nearly 300 square feet of reflected light shimmering into the dark corners. Obviously in principle they would work, but Udaipur proved that they were manageable.

Jim O'Brien, who shares the direction of the fourteen episodes and whose furthest point east until now had been Germany, found himself immediately plunged into the particular pressures of India when he began filming in the streets of Udaipur. A friendly group of a thousand spectators crowded in on every scene. It seemed impossible to keep them out of shot without using the police, and then it was almost impossible to keep out the police. Yet in intention the spectators could not have been more cooperative, keeping quiet during every take and bursting into applause the moment Jim said 'Cut'. Jim had been on the last of the

Geraldine James (above) and Tim Pigott-Smith.

LEFT
On location near Simla, with Ray Goode's reflector dominating the scene.

three recces with Christopher Morahan, and it took him no time to acquire a special feeling for India – he plans now to return on his own for a longer and less harassed visit. Yet an incident that same week in Udaipur did give him a disturbing glimpse of another side of Indian life.

For a scene in a temple Jim required several beggars as extras. They would merely sit in the open courtyard, soliciting alms. Priscilla John and Susie Bruffin, responsible for 'local casting', had found a suitable group of beggars living together on a particular street corner. Negotiations had been conducted through interpreters, and it had been agreed that these very specialized extras were to be collected by coach and taken to a temple outside the town for the filming. When the coach arrived to collect them, two problems arose. The Indian driver refused to take such people into his vehicle, and the beggars themselves said they had changed their minds and would not be coming. The second objection seemed insuperable until the reason was discovered. Somehow the rumour had spread that the filming was a sham and that they were to be carried off to a hospital where they would be sterilized by vasectomy. As Jim points out, their fears were themselves alarming. Eventually they were persuaded that the film was genuine, and then the only remaining problem was that they could not understand why the actors, visiting the temple in take after take, did not give them money as they squatted there. Their precious white and blue cards, saying GRANADA TV EXTRA and exchangeable at the end of the day for a relatively massive thirty or forty rupees, were far less reassuring than one or two tiny coins in the palm.

For Christopher Morahan, who shares the direction of the series and is the overall Producer, filming in Udaipur was an even sweeter moment, a transformation of dream into reality, for it was in these very streets, on the first day of his first recce, that India had made its initial impact on him. He had been walking alone through the city in the early morning. The Indian day was just beginning. Animals were arriving from the countryside with fresh produce. Donkeys plodded

along on their dainty hooves beneath great paniers of vegetables. A camel passed with slow disdain, on its way to some distasteful engagement, its soft feet, in such contrast to the donkey's, squidging on to the road like suction pads. Slatted metal shop fronts were sliding up to reveal tradesmen, sleepy-eyed after a night among their wares. Fires were being fanned, tea was on the brew, the day's gossip was slowly beginning. Christopher felt overwhelmed by a desire to capture on film, in the service of Paul Scott's books, this extraordinarily rich, vivid, ancient culture and our own alien reaction to it and influence upon it. Now, a year later, he was back in the same streets doing precisely that.

Christopher remembers with particular pleasure another moment halfway between those two times in Udaipur, and halfway also between dream and reality. He had returned from his recce with many photographs of the buildings and streets which he had chosen – together with Bill Shephard and with Vic Symonds, the Designer of the series – to represent the houses and scenes of Paul Scott's story. He spread out the photographs for Sir Denis Forman, who knows India better and had known the novels longer than the other members of the production team, and he sensed the excitement brought by this new step forward on the long road towards a completed series. Sir Denis had bought the rights to the four novels back in 1978. He had personally reorganized the scenes from Scott's complex fictional technique of multiple view and flashback into a chronological sequence more appropriate to television, and had made his own draft of the content of the fourteen separate programmes. Now, having for so long imagined each scene, he suddenly had before him the very steps up which Daphne Manners would stumble after being raped in the Bibighar Gardens, the Kashmiri houseboat in which her aunt would look after Daphne's baby, or the street in which Daphne's Indian lover would live an impoverished and obscure life in contrast to his English public-school background.

Scott's novels require four radically different Indian locations, each of them a typical part of life during the Raj. The fictional Mirat is a city of palaces, represent-

OPPOSITE LEFT
An extra with the card which by the end of the day will be worth some forty rupees.

OPPOSITE BELOW
Jim O'Brien (in the white cap) directing the scene at the temple near Udaipur, Susan Wooldridge on the left.

ABOVE
Producer and director at work in the streets of Udaipur—Christopher Morahan on the right, Jim O'Brien on the left.

RIGHT
Eric Porter in character as
Count Bronowsky.

BELOW
One of the black umbrellas,
providing some relief from the
heat of Mysore, with
Christopher Morahan, Susan
Wooldridge and crew.

ing one of the many states within British India which were left under the nominal control of their princely rulers. Udaipur was the location which emerged during Morahan's recces as the ideal candidate for Mirat. Its white marble palaces would make a perfect setting for the sophisticated machinations of the *émigré* Count Bronowsky, played by Eric Porter, who is adviser to the local ruler, the Nawab of Mirat. Eric's most vivid Indian memory is of wandering alone in the streets of Udaipur, observing but as far as possible unobserved. He was condemned to stroll abroad in a persona, that of Count Bronowsky, some twenty years older than his own, for back in England his hair had been bleached for the part. According to the names on the packets of dye, the make-up department had tried him out as 'intoxicating ivory', had modified that to 'silent snow' and had finally settled on 'secret silver'. This subtle hue had turned bright green when Eric swam in the hotel pool in Delhi – an unforeseen effect of chlorine – so the treatment was repeated and swimming-pools became out of bounds. But secret silver sounds an apt disguise for an unobtrusive observer of everyday life in an Indian street, that infinitely varied scene which Eric found 'far better than a film'.

Udaipur also provided some of the locations for Scott's Mayapore and Pankot, two towns with a strong British presence, both military and civil. Any details of these places not easily found in Udaipur were discovered in Mysore, a city further to the south and, as everyone was soon to discover, very much hotter. By contrast, Scott's Pankot is a hill station of the type used by the British to escape from the summer heat of the Indian plains. Simla, which from 1865 to 1939 was India's summer capital, provided all that was required for Pankot. Finally, several of Scott's scenes are set in Kashmir for which there is no substitute. So Udaipur, Mysore, Simla, Kashmir – this sequence of places was established on the recces, was confirmed on Sir Denis Forman's desk, and was followed through on location as the four stages of the production in India, occupying the period from 20 January to 8 May 1982.

While at Udaipur cast and crew had become acclimatized to much that is common in the east, such as the profusion of wild life. Bias against the taking of any form of life, combined with the heat of the climate, means that India is the swarming paradise of which ecologists dream. Everyone who travels there gets used to sharing many of the facilities with bugs and rodents. They feature frequently in the diary kept by Milly Preece, officially called Associate Producer but in fact the person responsible for the smooth running of the company's daily life, from problems of food and accommodation to more subtle matters of health and psychology. Milly was a sort of friendly regimental sergeant-major, operating without any of the usual weapons of bark or bite, and it would have been her problem if the cast had reacted badly to the vermin. Instead she was most impressed by the general air of calm. She kept a diary of the entire trip (on which much of my own account is based), and her entry for 16 February includes this evocative scene:

There were a couple of rather unwelcome guests in the dining room tonight. Two rats running round the soup tureens. I'm amazed at how calmly everyone accepts these things now. Judy Parfitt's comment on the matter was: 'You'd think the management would provide them with a separate dining room!'

The move down to Mysore in early March brought the first problems with the climate. The schedule had been fixed to catch the last of the relatively cool weather in the plains and the first of the spring warmth in the hills, but in the event the production ran into an unusually early heat wave in Mysore and an unusually late cold spell in Simla. With Mysore temperatures in the high nineties, Milly spent her time urging people to keep their heads covered until the last possible moment for a take, her pleas reinforced by those of the company medic, Dr Krishna, inevitably known to one and all as Harry. Their advice had little effect until people started passing out. Milly eventually found the answer in a bulk purchase of black umbrellas, which made the unit look like a funeral party huddled round the grave in bad weather. On one day, with a temperature of 104°F (40°C), the company's

ABOVE
Simla, the summer capital of
British India and the prototype
of every hill station.

RIGHT
Producer and Associate
Producer—Christopher
Morahan and Milly Preece on
location in Simla.

consumption of soft drinks and purified water topped 200 gallons. And yet a month later, in Simla, filming would be delayed by snow, everyone would spend the evenings round ineffectual coal fires, and two of the most distinguished members of the cast, Dame Peggy Ashcroft and Rachel Kempson, would wait in bed with hot-water bottles to be called for their next scene. On one occasion, determined to preserve at all costs their dwindling reserves of heat, they even bundled into the same bed.

Almost exactly fifty years before, in the summer of 1933, Rachel Kempson was playing Juliet at Stratford while Peggy Ashcroft played Juliet at the Old Vic. Their two fine roles in *The Jewel in the Crown* and their two superb performances somehow reflect the special quality of a long and brilliant career as a performer. Actors are capable of sustained achievement possible in few other professions, and clearly half a century of infinitely varied characterization leaves the eye keener than ever in the important matter of spotting a good part. Dame Peggy's claiming of Barbie Batchelor provides a delightful vignette in the production story of the series. During 1980 Christopher Morahan, then an Associate Director of the National Theatre, was using the telephone at the stage door to discuss some aspect of filming Paul Scott's 'Raj Quartet'. Dame Peggy happened to pass by and to overhear. She used the stage whisper of an old pro to make abundantly clear her single line: 'I want to be in it.'

Morahan was so surprised that he instantly rang off and turned to her: 'What did you say?'

Dame Peggy already knew and loved the books. She even knew which part was hers. She came straight to the point. 'I want to be Barbie Batchelor.' And so she is. And so she was waiting to be when she lay curled up in bed with her hot-water bottle in the foothills of the Himalayas.

Film crews abroad in Europe or the USA are accustomed to being able to telephone home, whether for professional or personal reasons. In India, where an internal call between major cities can take hours to achieve, this was clearly out of the question. So everyone had to rely on telex, itself very erratic in Indian hotels but capable of achieving a dialogue of sorts if there is an operator on the machine at the other end. In the fat bundles of telexes now in the Granada files, messages about film stock and rushes and transfer of funds are interspersed with more human details. A wife left at home wants urgent advice as to whether she should accept an offer on the house. A long list of Valentine messages is tapped out in good time for distribution at the other end by 14 February. An actress still in England requests a change in her travelling date to India so that she can get married and fit in a honeymoon, eliciting a brusque telex response from Christopher Morahan: WHY CANT SHEBE MARRIED IN WEEK 30. And always there was the chance of a completely informal exchange developing, among the staccato batches of capital letters, for within its stilted limits telex is a genuine conversation between typewriters:

IM OFF FOR DINNER NOW   WE ARE GOING FOR CHINESE TONIGHT   SHOULD BE GOOD
BIBI FOR NOW AND LOVE TO EVERYBODY   PLS TELL CAROL THAT BILL HAS ARRIVED
SAFELY OK?
OK WILL DO AND ALL HAVE A LOVELY TIME YOU LUCKY SOANDSOSE
BIBI JEAN SEE YOU SOON
BIBI

Mail would come in batches every week and newspapers were on average ten days old when they arrived. Milly noted in her diary that they were reduced to shreds as they were passed from reader to reader, and she added: 'I'm amazed at how interested people can be in out-of-date news.'

Anticipating the inevitable lack of entertainment, Milly had laid her own plans to keep people amused. In the 300 crates air-freighted from Manchester there were cricket bats and bails and balls, badminton racquets and shuttlecocks, and even – Christopher Morahan swears – a shove-halfpenny board that was never unpacked. There were video sets for evening film shows, though the worn-to-a-frazzle

Dame Peggy Ashcroft (above) and Rachel Kempson.

cassettes hired in Delhi combined with the fluctuating voltage in the hotels made these less than perfect entertainment. More successful were the sound tapes brought out for the regular Friday-evening discos. The ever-popular disc jockey was the production's Sound Recordist, Martin Kay – in his late twenties and extraordinarily young to have landed such an important project as this fourteen-part £5 million series. Presented, according to the hand-written poster, by ITV – Indian Trading Ventures – the first of these weekly events was held on 29 January at Udaipur. That night Milly noted:

It was a very successful evening. All the cast joined in and everybody relaxed and had a good time. The strains of 'Rule Britannia' and 'There'll always be an England' could be heard floating across Lake Pichola as the Lake Palace mob made their way back to the hotel in the boat. It is very interesting how patriotic people become when they are a long way from home.

It was a theme which had also interested Paul Scott. On that same day, 29 January, there had been a birthday. One of the cast, Derrick Branche, was thirty-five, and he had been extremely surprised to be presented at lunch with a Parker pen inscribed 'Happy Birthday in India from Granada Manchester'. It was merely the first of twenty-five such pens that Milly had brought out. By the time of the departure from India on 7 May they had all been used. But birthdays were not the only cause for celebration. Somehow a bottle of Moët & Chandon was produced by the Production Managers in Simla when news came through on the telex that Ray Goode had been made a member of the British Society of Cinematographers, a much-prized distinction, for his work as Lighting Cameraman on *Brideshead Revisited*.

One man who saw less of India than he would have wished was the Cost Clerk, Walter Livesey. It was his job to deal with all day-to-day cash matters, paying the local bills and providing ready money for all necessities. It was therefore he, more than anyone, who experienced the particular quality of Indian bureaucracy. It was he who spent hours sitting in those most astonishing of institutions, Indian banks. When I asked Christopher Morahan for his least prepossessing image of India he specified, without hesitation, the ceiling fans idly blowing air down towards the vast skyscrapers of documents on any official's desk, all reduced by time and inattention to a uniform shade of brown. To Christopher this was an image. For Walter Livesey it became an environment. He spent his first three weeks on the subcontinent sitting in the State Bank of India trying to open on Granada's behalf a bank account – on the face of it a simple enough task, which according to the London branch had already been arranged. Walter finally emerged with his precious cheque-book, only to discover that people in other parts of India preferred to be paid in cash because a cheque drawn on a bank in faraway Delhi took three weeks to clear.

So Walter became familiar, in each new location, with the peculiar mixture of suspended animation and frenzied inactivity which gives Indian banks their special quality. The long queues of ordinary people waiting at every counter have the stillness of enforced patience. Slightly more privileged customers are allowed access to the area just beyond, where at each banker's desk several people seem to be discussing at the same time their separate problems. And all the while the peons or bank orderlies, still wearing the voluminous khaki shorts inherited from the British which feature so prominently in *The Jewel in the Crown*, pad about removing documents from one pile and slapping them down on another. From this environment, nostalgic in memory but enraging at the time, Walter would emerge with a suitcase full of notes to carry him through the next two days. Sometimes he walked out of the bank with 200,000 rupees – worth a massive £12,500 even at the conventional rate of exchange, but more nearly the equivalent of a quarter of a million pounds in relation to Indian wages. At Simla Walter had a stiff twenty-minute walk uphill to the hotel with his heavily laden case (the largest available note was 100 rupees). He amazed the bank manager by declining an escort, and frankly he amazes me. 'Never felt safer in my life,' he told me. It chimed with an impression of Jim O'Brien's, that the entire company was isolated within India by affluence and therefore tended to feel safer than in parts of London. 'We floated through India a foot above the ground.'

The prime mover of this entire enterprise, Sir Denis Forman, had incautiously observed back in Manchester that it was perfectly possible to get things done in India – you just had to be firm. In keeping with this confidence, during his visit to the production in India he undertook the important task of arranging an overdraft for the last week of filming. It was considered unwise to leave India with the Granada account in credit, for the money might prove as hard to rescue as any other hostage, but Walter Livesey had made no progress at all on this refinement. Sir Denis proposed to tackle the matter at the highest level, expecting to see it through in one or two brisk discussions. A week or more later he was admitting defeat, and was recommending that Granada pay their way through the final seven days with £100,000 of traveller's cheques.

Sir Denis Forman and Christopher Morahan in the marble setting of Udaipur.

His account of his adventures, written for private circulation within Granada, is hilarious but also strangely endearing – for in some inexplicable way Indian bureaucracy, when recollected in tranquillity, does have a certain mad charm. Sir Denis suffered the same string of broken promises, flawed applications and futile appointments as plain Mr Livesey. The only difference was that he spent his time sitting in more comfortable offices, that much courteous attention was paid to his knighthood (though he was variously called Sir George and Sir Derek as well as Sir Denis), and that he was invited, as if to while away the necessary delay, to an evening of Oxford and Cambridge graduates, a vintage car rally, a quail shoot and a reunion of officers from the Dehra Dun Military Academy, of which he had himself been the very young Commandant in 1945. His description of the whole experience was intended to justify, to impatient administrators back home in Manchester, the apparent ineffectiveness of their colleagues out in India. He concluded:

From the above it will be clear that Indian business methods are often compounded of bluff, procrastination, sloth, duplicity, ineptitude and an irresponsible desire to please at any cost. And you will see that no matter that you love India and Indians, as I do, you have to admit that they do things a little differently.

If Indian bureaucrats astonish by their talent for inaction, Indian craftsmen do the opposite. Any traveller in the East knows that when it comes to a practical matter of repair or maintenance, some ingenious solution will always be found. Granada carpenters stared in amazement as their counterparts made effective use of scrap timber that the British would merely throw away. On one occasion Vic Symonds, the Designer of the series, wanted the façades of some houses to be erected beside a gate. He asked his Indian contacts to get hold of plywood. They seemed surprised: 'Why plywood?' When he explained, one of them went into the nearby village and returned with a family of masons who immediately ran up a series of mud and brick facades exactly as required.

Soon almost the entire village had settled in nearby in the hope of providing any services. One task in particular must have astonished and delighted them. Alan Rutter, in charge of props, had bought a large number of charpoys (basic Indian beds, each consisting of a wooden frame with hempen rope threaded across it), but being new they looked out of place in the scene, which was set in a sanctuary for the dying. In a unique bargain, new beds for old, the villages provided their own beds and took possession of Alan's. The receipt for the transaction, authenticated by their several thumb prints, survives in Granada's files.

But the ingenuity could also, it seemed, be obstructive. The Mysore racecourse had been chosen for one scene because of its fine spread of turf. Vic Symonds had a hotel room overlooking the course, and a week before the scene was due to be filmed he was horrified to see a carpet of flame spread across the entire open area, reducing it to a uniform smouldering black. This was normal practice, he was assured, to encourage the grass. But it did mean that Granada had to pay a fortune to water the course, twenty-four hours a day for seven days, to restore it to the

necessary shade of green.

Sir Denis Forman had brought with him from England exciting plans for the
filming that would still remain to be done at home. Instead of fitting the interior
sets into general studios, as and when they might be available, he proposed a
massive new studio for the exclusive use of *The Jewel in the Crown*. The Granada
TV Centre in Manchester is in the old industrial sector of the city, where redbrick
Victorian warehouses now stand empty, peering forlornly into the murky waters
of the River Irwell. Sir Denis had with him the drawings and ground plans for
turning one group of these buildings, known as the Botany warehouse, into a
custom-built setting for his *Jewel*. There were detailed discussions with the two
directors and Vic Symonds about the exact specifications, giving a new edge to the
relatively dull prospect of many more months of work in England. And yet this
building was within a year to bring the production its blackest single day.

That disaster, happily, was far in the future. Meanwhile there was the stimulat-
ing, exhausting, enraging, unceasing effort to capture on film each of the Indian
scenes within the time available. The conversation in the production office was
almost invariably about which actor had or had not an upset stomach, a touch of
heatstroke or sunburn, a fever or a sleepless night, and about the necessary
changes to the schedule to accommodate these facts. The cast knew that large
sums of money and often dwindling reserves of patience depended on their
continuing health, so they picked their way among enticing but potentially
dangerous dishes with the care of soldiers in a minefield. Tim Pigott-Smith, a yoga

enthusiast in England, was delighted to find a class in steamy Mysore which would help him keep fit, yet this could hardly save him from a day or two out of action after being poisoned by the hotel swimming pool. Even with all Geraldine James's care to ward off the sun, it found one day a chink in her armour and seared the tip of her nose so conclusively that she could not appear before the camera for several days. Milly's diary is full of brave invalids rising from their sickbeds and struggling into make-up and costume. None of this shows in the finished version, and the actors assure me that once the camera starts turning the illness mysteriously vanishes. It is an automatic cure known in the theatre, apparently, as Dr Floorboards.

At Simla the demons in charge of the weather surpassed themselves, providing snow and then day after day of thunderstorms. But whoever was dogging *Jewel* with good luck provided the occasional 'glorious sunny day' (the phrase seems to leap off Milly's page to express the sense of relief), and there were just enough such days to complete the work. Even that blessing seemed likely to be withheld in Kashmir, the romantic crocus-strewn valley in the Himalayas which miraculously spreads out before one after a mountainous pass as though it were Shangri-la itself. This was the favourite corner of India for the Moghul emperors, and in its spring finery it could be expected to make a splendid and relatively easy last location. Yet the first day in Kashmir was like a parody of a filming disaster.

The road from the hotel to the location was under water and all the vehicles, including the one containing the all-important generator, got stuck in the mud up to their axles. Morahan relieved the tension by making a short light-hearted film about the efforts to extricate them. Once they were freed, cast and crew were ferried to work in a fleet of *shikharas* – the characteristic gondolas of the Kashmiri lakes, delight of all tourists, which have a cushioned seat in the centre beneath a throne-like canopy and are propelled from behind with a paddle like a large and brightly painted ping-pong bat. The lakes of Kashmir are full of these craft, going about their everyday business of transporting food and vegetables in addition to sightseers. They provided a new headache for those members of the crew responsible for traffic control. They had just managed to cope with the pressure of vehicles on the Indian roads, but now suddenly the highway was hundreds of yards of water. It was impossible to dissuade the *shikhara* wallahs from paddling in and out of shot. And yet somehow, eventually, the scenes were in the can –

peaceful scenes of apparently unruffled conversation on two of the famous houseboats of these lakes, Kashmir's answer to hotels, each one as large and as well appointed with furniture, staff and interconnecting suites of rooms as any bungalow ashore. The *shikhara* attached to one of the houseboats was officially renamed by its owner 'Jewel in the Crown' – a canny move which for many years ahead will stimulate conversation, add a touch of glamour and no doubt improve profitability.

By Wednesday 5 May, on schedule, only three short sequences remained to be filmed. The last was completed just before lunch. It was a touching little scene at the graveside of Daphne Manners, the girl who dies giving birth to a child half Indian and half English. The element of farewell, of a brief meeting between two cultures coming now to an end, affected the real people present as much as the fictional characters. Milly records the event:

Rachel [Rachel Kempson, playing Daphne's aunt] looked wonderful in a huge hat with a veil over her face and the scene with the Ayah [the Indian nurse] putting flowers on Daphne's grave was lovely. Bill Roberts had saved a rocket specially for today and as Jim said 'Cut' for the last time, Bill set the rocket off. There was a strange atmosphere at lunch today. Nobody could quite believe that it was all over and that we'd made it through nearly four months in India and were now on our way home. Our adventures had come to an end.

Shikharas in the spectacular Kashmir landscape.

24

The return home was an end to the great eastern adventure, but it was very far from being an end to the production or the hard work. Indeed more than half the filming remained – a year ahead and only four months done – bringing obvious dangers of anticlimax and exhaustion. But there were many diversions to avoid monotony, among them the task of recreating parts of India in England. On the recces no place had been found which fulfilled all the needs of the Bibighar Gardens, where Daphne Manners is raped in the incident which casts its shadow over Paul Scott's entire story. It turned out to be simpler to create the necessary details of the garden in a disused Lancashire quarry.

For a different reason an important railway sequence had not been shot in India. The shattering climax of *The Jewel in the Crown* is an incident reflecting the communal riots at the time of partition, in 1947, when more than two million Indians were killed in clashes between Muslims and Hindus. Many of the worst massacres occurred on trains, as Muslims tried to escape into Pakistan or Hindus into India, and there is just such an act of butchery in the final episode of the series. Morahan decided that it would be unwise to stage anything so politically sensitive within India, where the memory of those appalling times is still fresh and where violence between the two groups has often flared up since. He may have erred on the side of caution, for in the interim Sir Richard Attenborough would film just such scenes in India for *Gandhi,* but the result was that the disused station of Quainton, in Buckinghamshire, was transformed into an authentic corner of India.

All the details, from the platform waiting room to the carriages of the train itself, were painstakingly recreated from photographs of the time – early on in the project Granada advertised for such photographs from old India hands and had a massive response. Many props used on location in India had travelled back with the company and were now in service again, including even a rickshaw. And the employment agencies of Luton, Watford, Aylesbury and Oxford yielded up 130 people of Indian origin to provide both the passengers on the train and the mob lying in wait. They were issued with dhotis and were shown how to wrap the length of white cloth round the body and between the legs before being tucked in at the waist (the majority had never worn a dhoti before), and then, under the direction of Jim O'Brien, they set about recreating the massacre. Jim tells me that he received only one moral objection to the distasteful work in hand. A man who could claim the title of Hajji – he had been on pilgrimage to Mecca – refused to pretend to be dead on the grounds that this was out of the question for anyone with that distinction. As a compromise, he agreed to be severely wounded. It was only a few months previously that an equally bemused collection of Europeans, working in the vicinity of Mysore, had been gathered together to play the guests at a wartime social occasion and had hobbled about in high-heel shoes of the 1940s and a temperature of 40°C, vastly enjoying themselves in spite of the developing blisters.

The laborious gathering-together of English extras in India and Indian extras in England raises the interesting question of how it was decided which scenes should be filmed in which place. The factors influencing this decision were complex. They might be reasons of tact, as in the case of the massacre. They might be practical; if an actor appears in only two scenes it is uneconomic to fly him out to India and those two scenes become strong candidates for an English location. They might be atmospheric: it is hard to recreate an entire bustling Indian street without it having the staged look of Hollywood exteriors of the 1930s. On the other hand it is easier to control the shooting of an interior if it is built in the studio, with gaps in the walls in convenient places and a ceiling replaced by lights. And so, for example, the outside of the MacGregor House was found and filmed in Mysore but the interior was created in Manchester. An actor arriving for a party would step out of his car in India and step through the front door in Lancashire. A ball was even bounced by a child in India and was caught in England by Charles Dance, playing Sergeant Perron. To match perfectly the lighting conditions, Ray Goode brought back to England details of the time of day, the compass orientation of each window for an interior, and the light level outside.

Apart from the visual aspects of scenery and atmosphere, there was one other important reason why as many scenes as possible should be filmed in India. A direct experience of Indian life, however brief or curtailed, enormously helped the actors in their characterizations. Several of the cast, pestered beyond endurance by the clutching hands and enquiring faces of an Indian crowd, were ashamed but enlightened to find themselves reacting with the dismissive gestures of the Raj, an attitude and a theme central to Scott's novels. So crucial was this experience of the country that Tim Pigott-Smith, in the calmer working patterns of England, would often go through his bundles of Indian photographs just to remind himself of the realities behind the fiction.

Back in Manchester, everyone was grateful for the calm of Botany. The old warehouses by the river had been transformed into a massive single enclosed space (in film jargon a 'four-wall situation') capable of housing at least three different sets at once so that filming could continue uninterrupted. The sense of measured calm was increased by the fact that the Granada canteen was only a three-minute walk away, and it became a familiar sight to see sepoys and turbanned bearers sitting down to lunch with British army officers in a manner unthinkable in the world they were together recreating. But on 26 January 1983 this calm was brutally shattered.

Only that afternoon I had been watching a scene in Botany – it was a cocktail party in the apartment of a Maharanee in Bombay – and filming had gone on until 6.00 p.m. By 7.15 there were flames fifty feet high leaping from the Botany roof, watched with horror from the nearby Granada offices by many of those involved in the production. No one was hurt and nobody knows how the fire started, but those gigantic flames were feeding on the sets and the props and the costumes

OPPOSITE ABOVE
Botany ablaze.

OPPOSITE BELOW
The Udaipur extras, being prepared for a massacre by Christopher Morahan.

ABOVE
After the massacre, on the adapted station platform at Quainton.

which were the background reality of many separate scenes in *The Jewel in the Crown*. The sets could be rebuilt in some other four-wall situation, and soon they were. To replace the many pieces of furniture with near-twins, close enough to avoid transgressing the shibboleth of continuity, it would be necessary to comb the antique shops armed with a sheaf of still photographs. This too was done. And the costumes were rapidly recreated. Strangely enough it was one single object – the artificial arm worn in the later episodes by Captain Merrick – which most nearly caused a problem. But a replacement was rushed through from Roehampton. And so, with a rapid reshuffling of schedules and a lasting regret for the convenience of their own private Botany, the production team was able to keep the show on the road with only the briefest of delays.

That was a tragedy surmounted. There was one other tragedy, a missing presence rarely noticed or commented upon but underlying the whole long process of production, to which there was no solution. When Paul Scott was writing these superb books, they were known only to the handful of people who keep abreast of new fiction. During the period when they were being published (1966-75) I believe that the average intelligent reader, asked to name the leading English novelists, would have come up with a dozen or even a score of names before reaching Paul Scott, if indeed reaching him at all. Then, in 1977, Scott won the Booker Prize with *Staying On*, a delightful but undeniably slighter work. Suddenly his name was everywhere, as a vast number of new readers were led by *Staying On* to discover the earlier books making up the 'Raj Quartet' – the very process by which Sir Denis Forman came to know the books, buying the rights first to *Staying On* and then to the four novels which have become *The Jewel in the Crown* (originally the title of the first part of the 'Raj Quartet').

Scott died in 1978 at the age of only fifty-seven and at the very moment when he was beginning to reach a wider audience. A fourteen-hour version of his Quartet on television is a culmination of that process and will send many new readers to his books – some of them no doubt only to find themselves baffled by his very complex fictional techniques after the straightforward narrative of the television series. Christopher Morahan told me that he would have loved to have Paul Scott beside him on the series, to guide him through many difficult points of interpretation or intention. And I have no doubt at all that Paul Scott would have loved to be there.

⚜3⚜

The Jewel in the Crown
EPISODE OUTLINES

by KEN TAYLOR

EPISODE ONE — *Crossing the River*

India, February 1942. On a bank of the river which divides the native and British communities in the town of Mayapore, a young Indian is found apparently dead by Sister Ludmila, an expatriate Russian who cares for the poor. She has him carried to her Sanctuary, where he is found in fact to be only dead drunk. Next morning Sister Ludmila has an unwelcome visit from Police Superintendent Ronald Merrick in search of a wanted man. It is a time of tension in India. The Japanese army is at the gates, following the British defeats in Malaya and Burma; Gandhi has called on his supporters not to assist the British war effort. Merrick at once takes a special interest in the young Indian, who claims in perfect English that he cannot understand his native tongue. His name is Hari Kumar and he is taken away for questioning after a violent altercation, but later released when it emerges that his uncle is a local merchant.

Hari resumes his work as a reporter on the *Mayapore Gazette* and thus meets Daphne Manners, a young voluntary worker at the British hospital, who has recently come to India having lost her family in England as a result of the war. Daphne is a gauche but sensitive girl who takes an immediate interest in Hari, discovering that he was brought up in England by his rich father and educated at a famous public school. Like her, he has been recently orphaned and finds himself in a strange land. Partly as a gesture against the rules, Daphne invites Hari to spend an evening with her at the MacGregor House where she is staying with Lady Chatterjee, a friend of her aunt Lady Manners. So Hari crosses the river from the poor Indian quarter where he lives and with the help of some dance-band records Daphne begins to build a bridge across the divide.

Superintendent Ronald Merrick is also an occasional visitor to the MacGregor House and one evening surprises Daphne by making a proposal of marriage. Despite an appeal to her sympathy when he explains that he is a rather isolated figure in British India with his humble background and education, Daphne turns him down. In some way Merrick repels her – though she is neither aware that he

29

and Hari have ever met, nor that Merrick is keeping a watchful eye on what he regards as their dangerous friendship.

The bond between Daphne and Hari Kumar strengthens when he invites her to visit the simple Indian house where he lives with his Aunt Shalini. Daphne responds to Aunt Shalini's affection for Hari, learning something of his very different life at an English public school and of his close friendship there with a boy named Colin Lindsey. Hari also tells her about Sister Ludmila's work at the Sanctuary, where Daphne now begins to give occasional help – though he does not disclose how he was once brought there himself. Only to Sister Ludmila does he confess that his drunkenness that night resulted from a meeting with Colin Lindsey on the cricket field in Mayapore, when Colin apparently failed to recognize the black face of his old school friend.

Cycling home together, Daphne and Hari are caught in a monsoon downpour and shelter in the Bibighar Gardens, the ruins of an Indian palace. It is a place of ghosts and here their friendship deepens into an unspoken love. Ronald Merrick, in his official role as Police Superintendent, now takes an opportunity to advise Daphne against continuing this dangerous relationship across the racial barrier. She reacts angrily and with a contempt which shocks him. He warns her of the growing tension in India, where Gandhi has called on his followers to 'do or die' in the struggle against British imperialism. Daphne ignores him and persuades Hari to show her the local Hindu temple – but on the night of their visit she finds he has become strangely antagonistic. They have a furious row when she discovers that he and Merrick have once clashed in circumstances which explain their mutual hostility, and which Daphne believes they have both concealed from her.

Congress leaders are now arrested and riots break out. In the hospital Daphne comforts an elderly missionary, Miss Crane, who has been attacked by bandits on the road. Amongst her luggage Daphne finds a curious allegorical painting of Queen Victoria sitting on an Indian throne – 'The Jewel in the Crown'. Later that night she visits the Sanctuary, hoping but failing to find Hari there. Merrick appears at the MacGregor House and asks Lady Chatterjee if she knows where Daphne may have gone. There have been outbreaks of violence in the district – and now Daphne appears to be missing.

EPISODE TWO — *The Bibighar Gardens*

Continuing his search for Daphne on a night of violence, Merrick arrives at the Sanctuary and questions Sister Ludmila, who lets slip the notion that Daphne might have called at Hari's house. Merrick drives there at once, goaded by a perverse sexual jealousy, but finds only Aunt Shalini. Meanwhile Daphne has stopped at the Bibighar Gardens while cycling home – and there she finds Hari. It is their first meeting since the quarrel and Hari tries to resist her hesitant attempts to cross the gulf between them, but in the darkness and under the spell of their physical proximity, desire suddenly overwhelms him and they make love.

Lady Chatterjee is speaking on the telephone to the Deputy Commissioner about Daphne's disappearance when a shout is heard from the garden and she returns – exhausted and dishevelled, collapsing on the verandah steps. Anna Klaus, the doctor, is called and Daphne tells them that she has been raped by a gang of ruffians in the Bibighar.

Merrick drives to the scene of the crime and finds Daphne's bicycle. In a hut by the level-crossing he also finds a group of Indian boys drinking hooch – one of them a friend of Hari's. On this evidence they are arrested and Merrick drives on to Hari's house, finding him blood-stained and partly dressed. In the police cells, Merrick subjects Hari to a long interrogation, naked and handcuffed. Refusing to answer questions, Hari is tied to a trestle and flogged, but will only say that he has not seen Daphne since the night they visited the temple – remaining loyal to a promise she has forced from him in a clumsy attempt to avoid his involvement.

Following the arrest of the Bibighar victims, as they are now known, riots break out in Mayapore. There are reports that Daphne's bicycle was found by the police near Hari's house and it is widely believed that the evidence is rigged. The Deputy Commissioner tries to restore peace through a local guru, Pandit Baba, who once attempted to teach Hari to speak Hindi. But the Pandit refuses to co-operate with the authorities – whilst on the other side of the divide Daphne equally resists intense pressure to provide evidence which might incriminate Hari or his friends. Through the whole of the official investigation, she maintains her story that she was raped by a group of bandits, but steadfastly conceals that she and Hari had made love together in the Bibighar before they were both attacked and over-powered.

Hari and the other boys are eventually jailed under the Defence of India Rules – a blanket charge for want of evidence. Daphne discovers she is pregnant and prepares to face the future alone – hoping and believing that she will bear Hari's child.

Hari Kumar – found drunk in a ditch the previous night by Sister Ludmila and her helpers – takes in his new surroundings at the Sanctuary.

EPISODE THREE — *Questions of Loyalty*

Daphne visits the Sanctuary for a final meeting with Sister Ludmila before setting out for Kashmir to stay with her aunt, Lady Manners. After a difficult labour and a Caesarian operation, she dies here giving birth to her half-caste child. On board her houseboat on Lake Srinagar Lady Manners reads Daphne's journal, written under the premonition that she might die and apologizing for the burden she has inflicted on the aunt of 'that Manners girl'. Lady Manners has decided to bring up the child and to call her Parvati. As a senior member of the old Raj, she cares nothing for the hostility this will evoke in the British community.

Certainly this is felt by Mildred Layton on a nearby houseboat as she talks to her daughter Sarah. She is on holiday from her hill station Pankot, preparing for the wedding of her younger daughter Susan to an officer in the 'Muzzy' guides, Teddie Bingham, who has recently been posted to Mirat. Teddie has also acquired a new room-mate with a mysterious past. His name is Captain Ronald Merrick.

Merrick has apparently pulled strings to obtain a difficult transfer from the police to the military and is fast becoming an expert on the subject of the Indian National Army – Indian prisoners-of-war who have gone over to the Japanese to effect the liberation of India. Teddie is shocked by such treachery and wonders if there may be some connection with a strange discovery at his billet – cabalistic chalk marks on the floor and the brief appearance on the verandah of a rusted lady's bicycle. He consults Merrick, who remains equivocal. Merrick does, however, make practical suggestions to Teddie about arrangements for his marriage to Susan. The wedding must take place at once in Mirat before their imminent posting to the battle-front.

In Kashmir Sarah secretly pays a visit to Lady Manners' house-boat and sees the

OPPOSITE ABOVE LEFT
Daphne Manners on the verandah of the MacGregor house in Mayapore after her first day as a voluntary worker at the local British hospital.

OPPOSITE ABOVE RIGHT
Hari Kumar walks from the MacGregor house after meeting Daphne for the first time at Lili Chatterjee's cocktail party.

OPPOSITE BELOW LEFT
Meeting Hari Kumar in the cantonment bazaar, Daphne invites him to tea at the MacGregor house.

OPPOSITE BELOW RIGHT
Intending to have tea at the MacGregor house, Daphne and Hari cycle away from the bazaar towards the Bibighar Gardens.

BELOW
A hesitant Daphne enters the local temple with Hari and other worshippers to make puja.

Merrick, accompanied by police
officers, arrives to carry out a
search at Sister Ludmila's
sanctuary.

RIGHT
Hari carries the distraught
Daphne out of the Bibighar
Gardens after they have been
attacked and over-powered by
unknown assailants.

half-caste baby which was conceived as a result of the notorious rape-case. She is deeply affected by Lady Manners' wisdom and tranquillity and seeks her advice on a suitable gift for the family to make to the Nawab of Mirat, in whose guest-house the wedding party will be staying.

Back in Pankot the news of the rushed wedding arrangements is now broken by the Laytons to the girls' step-grandmother Mabel and to her houseguest, the ex-missionary teacher Barbie Batchelor. Barbie is evidently disappointed that she and Mabel will not now be able to attend. She is devoted to the two girls, but especially to Sarah – to whom she confides that her old friend Edwina Crane in Mayapore has recently committed suicide by burning herself to death in her garden shed. Barbie also has a copy of the picture 'The Jewel in the Crown', which Miss Crane used to teach the children English. Both she and Sarah seem haunted by the events in Mayapore a year ago during the riots.

EPISODE FOUR — *Incidents at a Wedding*

The Laytons' wedding plans are thrown into sudden confusion by the illness of the best man. Susan telephones Teddie in Mirat and tells him to cope with the emergency – which rather uncharacteristically he is able to do. He knows of a substitute – 'the fellow I share quarters with. He seems a helpful and willing sort of chap.' So Merrick becomes his best man.

The arrival of the wedding group in Mirat arouses the interest of the Nawab's Chief Minister, Count Bronowsky, an émigré Russian who has an eye for every

Daphne Manners comes to say goodbye to Sister Ludmila at the Sanctuary in Mayapore before leaving to join her Aunt before having her baby.

35

Rachel Kempson—Lady
Manners—at the Lake Nageen
location in Kashmir.

The camera crew manoeuvre
their *Shikharas* into position for
a shot of Lady Manners's
houseboat on Lake Nageen,
Kashmir.

detail – the other being obscured by an eye-patch acquired at some stage in his dramatic career. He questions his young secretary, Ahmed Kasim, the son of a leading Congress politician whom the British have now imprisoned. Ahmed is personally detached from politics, which later that evening involves him in a clash with another visitor to Mirat – Pandit Baba Sahib from Mayapore. Ahmed, however, has a certain interest in the previous year's events in the Bibighar Gardens and learns from Pandit Baba of the brutal treatment of the young detainees by the Police Superintendent at that time. Next morning he goes riding with Sarah, carefully preserving his distance from the English memsahib – which does not prevent Aunt Fenny from noting the event with disapproval and arousing Sarah's anger.

As Teddie and his best man are driving to the church in the Nawab's car, a more serious incident occurs. A stone is thrown and shatters the window, cutting Teddie's face. Bronowsky concludes that the gesture was made against the occupants of the car, not the Nawab. He also reports to his master that the name of one of the officers, Captain Merrick, is familiar to him for reasons which he cannot quite recall.

Fresh tensions arise at the reception when the Nawab is at first refused entry by the military police, though afterwards Susan charms him with her graceful curtsy and it seems that perhaps the day's disasters are at an end. But Count Bronowsky has now remembered the context in which Merrick's name is known to him. As Merrick returns from an errand, Bronowsky appears and forces from him the admission that since the rape case he has suffered a number of small acts of persecution, of which the stone throwing may be the latest. Merrick's response seems fatalistic. 'They can hardly follow where I'm going, unless some sepoy has

Sarah gallops towards the 'nullah' where Merrick has fallen from his horse during a challenge race with Ahmed.

Susan Layton – returning from
shopping in the bazaar – joins
her elder sister Sarah and their
mother Mildred on their
houseboat in Kashmir.

RIGHT
Mildred and her sister Fenny are
joined for breakfast by Sarah as
preparations continue for
Susan's wedding in Mirat.

OPPOSITE
Fabia Drake (left) and Peggy
Ashcroft rehearse a scene with
Christopher Morahan in the
garden of the Rose Cottage
location at Mashobra, Simla.

been bribed to put a bullet through my head.' But Merrick will not escape so simply from the consequences of that night in the Bibighar Gardens.

OVERLEAF
Daybreak over the houseboats of Lake Nageen.

EPISODE FIVE — *The Regimental Silver*

On Mirat station the wedding party is assembled to wave goodbye to Susan and Teddie as they leave for their honeymoon. An Indian woman in a white saree approaches Merrick and begins to plead with him, falling at his feet in tears. Sarah clutches the bridal bouquet as Merrick reacts with horror and the woman is led away by her companion. It is Pandit Baba – and the woman in white is Hari's Aunt Shalini.

That evening Merrick comes to the lakeside guest-house and finds Sarah alone. He wants to apologize for the embarrassment of his presence at the wedding – 'I was the worst best man Teddie could have chosen.' Sarah questions him about the rape case and he reveals that he senses a similarity between her and Daphne, although Sarah's response to the Anglo-Indian problem is more complex. She

OPPOSITE ABOVE LEFT
Under the expert eye of his falconer, Ahmed prepares Mumtaz for a morning's hawking.

OPPOSITE ABOVE RIGHT
Jim O'Brien (left) with his camera team Jon Woods (right) and Lawrence Jones shoots the closing sequence of the series from a Dakota aeroplane over the aerodrome at Mysore.

OPPOSITE BELOW LEFT
Jim O'Brien explains the action of a scene filmed in Mysore involving Nicholas Farrell and a motorcyclist extra.

OPPOSITE BELOW RIGHT
Members of the crew and cast make an early morning departure from the Lake Palace Hotel for filming in Udaipur.

LEFT
Shooting on the Laytons' holiday houseboat in Kashmir.

BELOW
Recreation of Mayapore's War Week Exhibition on the racecourse at Mysore.

ABOVE
Sarah, accompanied by Count
Bronowsky, meets the Nawab
at his palace in Mirat.

OPPOSITE ABOVE
The Nawab, accompanied by
Count Bronowsky and Ahmed,
is refused entry to Susan and
Teddie Bingham's wedding
reception at Mirat's Gymkhana
Club.

OPPOSITE BELOW
The town of Simla – one of the
four main Indian locations.

dislikes him instinctively and knows that he is probing for a link between her and Ahmed Kasim.

Merrick and Teddie leave for the war-front on the borders of Burma and Susan returns with her family to their hill station at Pankot. Her father, Colonel Layton, is a prisoner-of-war in Germany and there are hidden tensions between her mother, Mildred, and his step-mother. Mabel Layton is living in Rose Cottage, the family home, while Mildred and her daughters are crowded into an army grace-and-favour bungalow. Barbie Batchelor, the ex-missionary who lives with Mabel, feels that as an interloper she has become the focus of this problem. But she is devoted to Mabel and deeply involved in all family affairs. She talks perceptively to Sarah about Merrick and the Manners rape case, presenting her with a set of silver apostle spoons, a wedding gift to Susan.

Meanwhile in Ranpur Lady Manners has persuaded the Governor to review the evidence against Hari Kumar and watches in secret as he is questioned at the Kandipat jail. Hari describes Merrick's obscene advances to him whilst he was being flogged and finally weeps when he hears that Daphne has died in childbirth. Both Lady Manners and the examining officer believe his story. They think he will now be released, but that the evidence against Merrick will be suppressed.

Mabel and Barbie are invited to Susan's combined wedding and twenty-first birthday party in the Officers' Mess, a symbolic moment for Mabel, who has mixed feelings about her long attachment to the regiment. Barbie searches for her silver

BELOW
Jim O'Brien directs Nicholas Farrell as Teddie Bingham in a sequence filmed in Udaipur.

Make-up supervisor Anna Jones puts the finishing touches to Tim Pigott-Smith's complicated make-up for the scene in which Ronald Merrick and his men are ambushed in the Burma jungle.

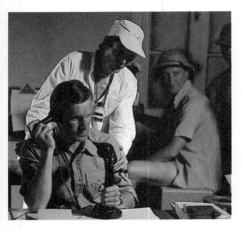

RIGHT
In the Burma jungle Ronald Merrick and Teddie Bingham interrogate the captured Indian National Army soldier Mohammed Baksh.

OPPOSITE
Merrick drags Teddie Bingham from the blazing jeep after the ambush in the Burma jungle.

spoons amongst the display of wedding presents – and finds they are missing. This troubles her greatly and increases her sense of Mildred's hostility.

Sarah works as a WAC(I) corporal at the barracks and is thus the first member of the family to be given the tragic news that Teddie has been killed in action. She has to break it to Susan, who is now several months pregnant. Susan's response reflects her own damaged personality – outwardly bright and attractive, but deeply insecure. After an outburst of wild hysteria she withdraws into her inner life, sheltering behind the conventional mask of a young war widow.

EPISODE SIX — *Ordeal by Fire*

Susan receives the official letter which gives an account of Teddie's death. She talks to Sarah of her reactions, telling her she feels exposed like an insect revealed by an upturned stone. She wants Sarah to go to Calcutta to see Merrick who was wounded in an heroic attempt to rescue Teddie from the action in which he died. Sarah is reluctant to be further involved with a man she instinctively dislikes, but as always she is forced to suppress her own feelings.

In the European bazaar before setting out, Sarah has a brief glimpse of Lady Manners in her old-fashioned solar topee – reminding her of their meeting on the lake in Srinagar and of Daphne's half-caste child. She talks about this to Barbie, her only confidante, when she calls at Rose Cottage to say goodbye. In response to another of Susan's requests, she also asks Mabel to give her the old family christening gown for Susan's expected baby. It is made of delicate lace in a butterfly pattern and Mabel has already promised Barbie a remnant of the same precious material as a legacy.

In Calcutta Sarah is shocked to find that Merrick has been seriously burned and

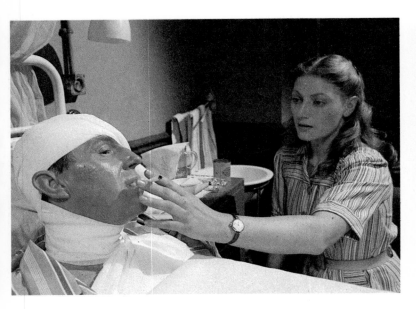

ABOVE
In a Calcutta hospital, Sarah listens to Ronald Merrick explain how Teddie Bingham died when both were caught in a jungle ambush.

ABOVE RIGHT
Sarah comforts her sister Susan when the news of her husband Teddie's death reaches Pankot.

RIGHT
From the doorway of Rose Cottage, Barbie, Nicky Paynton, Mildred Layton and Clara Fosdick watch as Sarah breaks the news of Teddie Bingham's death to Susan, his wife.

injured in the incident which resulted in Teddie's death. He tells her how Teddie
walked into a Japanese ambush, foolishly accepting the story given to him by a
captured deserter – a sepoy from Teddie's regiment who had joined the INA.
Merrick as an expert on the subject distrusted the sepoy's story, but Teddie was
swayed by his faith in the traditions of Indian Army service. In some way his
death reminds Merrick of the suicide by burning of Miss Crane in Mayapore with
her picture of Queen Victoria on an Indian throne – a vision of the old Raj which
is now going up in flames. As Sarah leaves the hospital she learns that he is to have
an operation next day for the amputation of his left arm.

In Calcutta Sarah is staying with Aunt Fenny who at first assumes that her visit
has been prompted by a romantic interest in Merrick. 'A Board school boy, Aunt
Fenny?' Sarah comments, 'with only one arm. Couldn't I do better than that?'
Despite the savage irony, Fenny persists in hoping for some solution to what she
regards as Sarah's problem. A more likely candidate appears to be one of the
young officers who have been attending the course run by Uncle Arthur and who
are dining at the flat. The Allied invasion of Europe has just been announced and
the young men are keen to go dancing if Sarah will join them. Jimmy Clark is
older and more sophisticated than the rest. During the evening he persuades
Sarah to leave the dance-floor and to set out with him alone. 'Where are we
going?' she asks as he leads her off into the night. 'Across the so-called bridge,'
Clark tells her. 'It's what you have to cross to reach the other side.'

An evening of Indian classical
music is provided at the home
of Mira, rich and sophisticated
friend of Major Clark.

EPISODE SEVEN — *Daughter of the Regiment*

Clark takes Sarah to the house of his rich and sophisticated Indian girl-friend, subjecting her to an evening of culture-shock as a result of which he finally seduces the 'colonel's daughter' who has so far clung to her virginity. But Sarah knows she will never be part of his cynical brave new world. The Raj has made her and she belongs – 'that's the trouble.'

On this night too at Rose Cottage, Barbie slips into Mabel's bedroom to ensure that all is well before she goes to sleep. Mabel is in a mood to talk – remembering her first husband, beside whom she hopes to be buried, and the Amritsar Massacre in 1919 when the British fired on an unarmed Indian crowd. It happened at Jallianwallah Bagh and Mabel was moved to make a gesture in support of the bereaved families. Barbie feels especially close to her at this moment and in some way reassured that Mabel needs her – however much Mildred may resent her presence in Rose Cottage.

Next day she goes to visit her friend the organist of the garrison church, leaving Susan resting on the verandah while Mabel works in the garden which she cherishes. Later Susan wakes to find Mabel apparently asleep in the opposite chair, still wearing her old gardening hat. The vicar comes to bring Barbie the half-expected news that her friend is dead.

Barbie returns to Rose Cottage and finds that Susan has gone into premature

ABOVE
During a break in a long musical evening, Sarah is shown round the luxurious Calcutta house by her hostess Mira.

RIGHT
Sarah and her escort Major Clark together during Mira's musical evening.

OPPOSITE
Filming of a scene on a mountain road outside Simla.

BELOW
Ahmed on horseback at Pratap,
near Udaipur.

OPPOSITE
Barbie pleads with the
unflinching Mildred for Mabel
to be buried in Ranpur
alongside her first husband.

labour from the shock of Mabel's death. Mildred has taken charge and has locked away all Mabel's possessions. The station adjutant, Captain Coley, is also there and he informs Barbie that Mabel's body has been removed to the hospital. With grim determination, Barbie sets out to ensure that her friend's remains will be properly laid to rest.

Shocked by the sight of Mabel's corpse in the mortuary, Barbie penetrates into the private bedroom where Mildred is staying while Susan is in labour. Mildred is slightly drunk, a state which has become habitual during the time her husband has been a prisoner-of-war. A bitter conflict develops between the two women – Barbie passionately convinced that Mabel will only be at peace when she is buried beside her first husband, and Mildred accusing her of a vulgar intrusion into private and family affairs. 'You were born with the soul of a parlour-maid. India's been very bad for you and Rose Cottage a disaster. I'd be glad if you'd be out of there by the end of the month.' Finally to silence her pleading, Mildred empties a jug of water over Barbie's head.

Sarah is travelling home from Calcutta, having heard the news of Mabel's death. It is the first train journey she has made alone and, despite her sadness, she feels a sense of challenge and excitement. The colonel's daughter has begun to free herself from the past.

ABOVE
Rehearsal of Barbie's return by
rickshaw to the empty Rose
Cottage to collect the tin trunk
holding her last few belongings.

OPPOSITE LEFT
June 1945: Barbie has spent
several months in the mission
hospital at Ranpur. Visiting her,
Sarah Layton finds that Barbie
has not spoken for weeks.
Outside the vultures circle the
Towers of Silence.

OPPOSITE RIGHT
Shrouded in her butterfly lace,
Barbie dies in the mission
hospital at Ranpur, August
1945.

EPISODE EIGHT — *The Day of the Scorpion*

On the station platform waiting for her connection to Pankot Sarah encounters
Count Bronowsky, the Nawab's chief minister whom she met in Mirat. Bronowsky
invites her to join him for a glass of champagne on the Nawab's special coach and
introduces her to Nigel Rowan, the young English officer who interrogated Hari
Kumar in prison. Bronowsky is on a mysterious mission – reflecting in his urbane
manner on the events at Susan's wedding, her husband's tragic death and the
injuries which he now learns Captain Merrick sustained in trying to rescue him.
He also recalls Sarah's morning ride with young Ahmed Kasim and claims to
notice a subtle change in her. 'How self-contained you are. I don't remember that.'

In fact, Bronowsky's mission is to conduct Ahmed under Rowan's supervision
to a meeting with his father – 'MAK' Kasim, the ex-chief minister of Ranpur. The
Governor has recently decided to release MAK from prison where he has been
detained like other Congress leaders since 1942. Ahmed has to break to his father
the news that Sayed, MAK's elder son, has been captured fighting alongside the
Japanese as a member of the INA. MAK is deeply shaken by the circumstances of
his own release and by Sayed's betrayal of his oath as a King's Commissioned
Officer. But Ahmed finally persuades him to come to terms with India's new
political realities.

By the time Sarah returns to Pankot, Susan's baby has been born and Mabel
buried – though not as Barbie believes she should have been. After her row with

Mildred, Barbie has left Rose Cottage and begun to move her possessions into a little room at the home of the vicar and his wife Clarissa. She is happy to see Sarah again, but even this relationship is bitterly tainted by Clarissa's hint that there may be something unnatural in Barbie's affection for the Layton girls. In the church where she has gone to put flowers on Mabel's grave, Barbie has a brief glimpse of Lady Manners – a vision of reconciliation between the old Raj and the new India which she takes for a sign of grace. Outside in the churchyard she is approached by a Hindu beggar boy. Barbie feels old and tired and far from home, but in this little unknown Indian she seems to sense a hope for India's future.

Briefly and secretly Merrick arrives in Pankot to recuperate at the military hospital after the fitting of an artificial arm. His burned face is still hidden, but he has determined not to disclose himself until he has mastered the control of his metal limb. Failure and pain incense him almost to the point of madness – but it is Susan whose hold on sanity now suddenly snaps. Re-enacting a long remembered ritual for dispatching a scorpion, she wraps her baby son in his christening gown of butterfly lace and surrounds the baby in a ring of burning kerosene, watched by her terrified young ayah. 'Free,' Susan intones. 'Little prisoner – go free!'

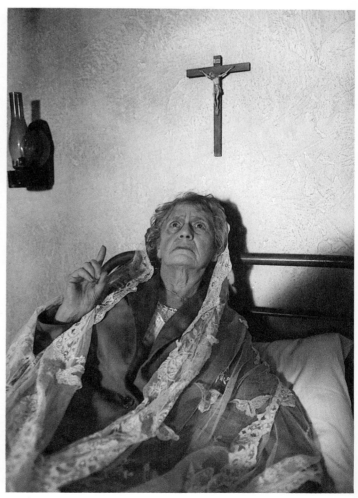

ABOVE
Geraldine James at Simla

RIGHT
Sunderban, Mashobra –
location of Rose Cottage.

OPPOSITE
Sunset over Lake Nageen,
Kashmir.

EPISODE NINE — *The Towers of Silence*

Susan's baby is snatched from death – but in Pankot hospital she seems to have drifted into mental isolation. The psychiatrist tells Sarah that Mildred blames Barbie for the breakdown, chattering about the christening gown being like butterflies caught in a web. Was Barbie important to her sister? 'Not really,' Sarah answers. 'Important to me.'

Mildred now returns Barbie's wedding gift of apostle spoons. 'Blessed are the insulted and the shat-upon,' Barbie informs the vicar's wife with whom she is lodging. She resolves to present the spoons instead to the Officers' Mess, arriving at the adjutant's house in a downpour. Hearing strange sounds, Barbie makes her way into the apparently empty house – and stumbles upon Mildred and Captain Coley making love. She runs out into the rain – and a few days later contracts pneumonia.

As a result of her own sexual initiation in Calcutta, Sarah is pregnant. She has no wish to see her lover again and arranges to go away to Aunt Fenny's for an abortion. Before leaving Pankot she comes to see Barbie, who is making a slow recovery in hospital. In a cracked voice she asks Sarah to arrange to store her trunk in the garden shed at Rose Cottage. There is no space for it in her little room. Sarah also promises to ask the director of the Calcutta Mission to find Barbie a job. Barbie has begun to fear that God has no further use for her.

With the help of her young psychiatrist, Susan makes her return to social life at a party and startles everyone with her apparent recovery. As Mildred leaves

with the area commander's wife, the car in which they are travelling is almost driven off the road by a limousine containing an old lady in a veiled solar topee, a young ayah and a half-caste girl. Nobody recognizes Lady Manners and Daphne's child making their way home.

An embarrassed Captain Coley is now forced to ask Barbie to remove her trunk from the garden shed at Rose Cottage. Barbie is happy to oblige. She has just had a letter informing her that there is a vacancy at the Dibrapur Infants' School. But when she reaches her old home she discovers a man on the verandah with a scarred face and a metal claw in place of his left arm. Ronald Merrick has come in search of the Laytons. As thunder rumbles around them, Barbie overcomes her fear and asks him about her dead friend Edwina Crane. He tells her that Miss Crane left a suicide note: 'There is no God, not even on the road from Dibrapur.' Barbie is filled with horror. 'It's where I'm going.'

Merrick helps her to load her heavy trunk onto the rickshaw and she sets off in more cheerful mood – but on the way down the steep hill the runners lose control and the rickshaw overturns, spilling Barbie onto the road. Months later, Sarah finds her in Ranpur mission hospital – clutching a length of butterfly lace. She seems unable to grasp that the war in Europe is over and Sarah's father is coming home. Outside her window the vultures circle the towers of silence where the Parsees expose their dead.

EPISODE TEN — *An Evening at the Maharanee's*

Bombay, 5 August 1945. Guy Perron, a peacetime university lecturer but now a sergeant in army intelligence, witnesses the interrogation of a returning Indian prisoner-of-war, a *havildar* suspected of collaborating with the INA in Germany. The examining officer is Major Merrick, DSO, who afterwards questions Perron and discovers that this good-looking young man was at school at Chillingborough and can remember there a boy named Hari Kumar. Merrick tells him that Hari came to a sticky end.

The other officer present is Captain Purvis, formerly an academic economist, who is struggling to cure his depression and chronic dysentery with alcohol. He sends Perron off with a bottle of rare Scotch whisky to a very unorthodox party in the flat of a beautiful Maharanee. Perron is to report back on any careless talk he overhears about the fleet which is assembling off-shore for the invasion of Malaya.

Amongst the strangely exotic crowd at the party, Perron meets Sarah Layton who has come to Bombay to welcome her father Colonel Layton, also a returning prisoner-of-war. With her are Count Bronowsky and young Ahmed Kasim – but, less happily for Perron, she is escorted by Ronald Merrick. Merrick is obviously intrigued by the young sergeant's appearance in this bizarre setting, for which Perron quite properly refuses to provide an explanation. He leaves with Bronowsky and the others when the party is suddenly disrupted by the Maharanee, who has declared that Perron's gift of whisky is poisoned.

Perron has realized that Sarah is staying with relations in the same block of flats as Captain Purvis, but when he returns he discovers that the drunken officer has attempted suicide by slashing his wrists in the bath. With Merrick's help, Purvis is rescued and dispatched to hospital. Sarah invites Perron to come down to her uncle's flat for a meal, though Merrick warns that there are two subjects which must not be discussed – the *havildar* and Hari Kumar.

Perron now meets Sarah's father, who has returned early from an evening out with Aunt Fenny and Uncle Arthur. Colonel Layton has clearly suffered as a prisoner-of-war and is easily tired. He is also concerned about one of his men – a *havildar* who has been accused of treachery. After he has retired to bed, Sarah persuades Merrick to go and reassure her father about the problem, though he tells her there is little he can do. Left alone, Sarah talks to Perron about his time at Chillingborough and asks him whether he remembers a boy named Hari Kumar. Perron is forced to be evasive.

Merrick has resolved that Perron shall join him in his task of rooting-out INA
suspects. He drops Perron off at his camp and remarks that he will see him again
in a couple of days' time. 'Oh, no, you won't,' Perron declares to the departing
taxi. 'You bloody well won't!'

EPISODE ELEVEN — *Journeys into Uneasy Distances*

The train which brings Sarah and her father home to Pankot snakes into the hills
with a carriage-load of wounded sepoys. It is 7 August 1945. A radioactive dust
cloud has settled over Hiroshima. In Ranpur mission hospital Barbie lies dead.

Sarah and Colonel Layton are welcomed by Captain Coley, who is now
rumoured to be looking for a new posting. After five years this is a rather strained
return to Rose Cottage for Colonel Layton, but the first sight of his new grandson,
Edward, helps to reunite the family. In prison camp he has heard little of their
anxieties. The Officer Commanding Pankot Rifles cannot yet face full exposure to
the outside world.

A few days after her return Sarah has a telephone call from Nigel Rowan – an
officer on the Governor's staff in Ranpur who has visited the mission hospital at
her request to collect a package which Barbie has apparently bequeathed to her.
Rowan is coming to Pankot on official business to visit ex-Chief Minister 'MAK'
Kasim, now in political purdah since his release from prison. An opportunity to
see Sarah is something Rowan welcomes.

On the station platform in Ranpur he has another encounter. A Lieutenant-
Colonel with a scarred face and a metal claw demands accommodation in the
Governor's special compartment. Merrick has with him an evil-looking servant
named Suleiman and an intelligence sergeant, whom Rowan immediately recognizes as an old school-fellow. Despite his resolution, Guy Perron has been
trapped. On the journey he paints for Rowan a vivid picture of Merrick's dia-
bolical influence, which has now brought about the suicide of the suspect *havildar*
belonging to Colonel Layton's regiment. Perron is determined to make his escape
and has already begun to pull strings in England for an early demob. He also
refers briefly to their mutual school-friend, Hari Kumar. Rowan has been keeping
an eye on Hari since his release, but he says nothing of this to Perron.

Neither Rowan nor Perron is aware that Merrick has made another important
conquest during the time he was in Pankot for the fitting of his metal arm. With

Colonel Layton's approval he is now about to be engaged to Susan. This news is broken to Sarah on a specially arranged morning ride with her father – a picnic breakfast, reviving an old pre-war habit. Sarah is horrified and alarmed. She has learned enough from Nigel Rowan to be deeply suspicious of Merrick's character. But her father attributes her response to natural jealousy and the emotional gulf remains between them.

Sarah turns to Rowan in a desperate attempt to prevent her sister's marriage, sensing that he knows more of Merrick's past than he has ever disclosed. But he retreats behind a wall of official silence. 'I'm sorry, Nigel. I shouldn't try to involve you. It's not your problem.' She fumbles to open the parcel which he has brought her – Barbie's legacy. A length of butterfly lace . . .

EPISODE TWELVE — *The Moghul Room*

15 August 1945. News reaches Pankot Area HQ of the Japanese surrender. Merrick is recalled to Delhi, leaving Perron to follow shortly and thus free to join his old school friend, Nigel Rowan, at the Summer Residence guest-house. Perron is delighted not only to be rid of Merrick, but also to escape from the hospital annexe where he is billeted and whose inmates have become mysteriously hostile. From Corporal 'Sophie' Dixon, one of the medical orderlies, he learns that this was due to his assumed links with Merrick and his Pathan servant Suleiman. Dixon describes how Merrick, when he was previously attending the hospital,

A grateful Nawab says goodbye to Sarah in the salon of his palace in Mirat.

61

contrived with Suleiman to blackmail a young homosexual orderly. Merrick was thus able to obtain details from the psychiatrist's records about one of his patients – a certain Mrs Bingham. From Nigel Rowan, Perron learns that this is the married name of Merrick's fiancée Susan, with whose family he and Rowan are to dine.

Later that night, in answer to his questions, Rowan gives Perron the file on Hari Kumar. He also bequeaths to him the use of the guest-house, which Rowan is vacating to return to his old job in Delhi in the political department.

With the war over, elections will soon be held and the government is anxious to enlist the help of ex-Chief Minister 'MAK' Kasim. A meeting is now arranged between him and his son Sayed, awaiting trial as an INA deserter from the Indian army. MAK is briefed by the officer in charge of Sayed's case, Lieutenant-Colonel Merrick, who takes this opportunity to probe the congressman about his own persecution at the hands of nationalist agitators. MAK instinctively dislikes him and warns Sayed to be on his guard against this officer who claims to be his friend. Sayed urges MAK as a Muslim to leave the Congress Party and to join the Muslim League, but his father refuses to accept the inevitability of an India divided between Muslims and Hindus. Later he talks to Ahmed about his political future, reaching an understanding with his younger son which he has only experienced in the past with Sayed.

Production designer Vic Symonds (centre) makes a final check of the train before shooting begins at Dubari, near Udaipur.

In Pankot, Perron receives the miraculous news that his wangled demobilization has come through. Better still – the arrangements are supervised by a WAC(I) sergeant, Sarah Layton. That night before he leaves the guest-house, he and Sarah talk of Hari Kumar and are suddenly drawn to one another – like Hari and Daphne on a similar night in the Bibighar Gardens. They visit the deserted Summer Residence and in the dust-sheeted Moghul Room they make love. Afterwards Perron watches Sarah disappear into the dark and remembers Hari's words: 'I haven't seen Miss Manners since the night we visited the temple.' Now he is leaving India – but not perhaps the ghosts of its past.

EPISODE THIRTEEN — *Pandora's Box*

2 August 1947. Guy Perron, now a Cambridge lecturer in history, returns to India on the eve of independence to observe the last days of the Raj. At Count Bronowsky's invitation he arrives in Mirat at a moment of crisis – not only in relations between the Muslim and Hindu communities, but also in the lives of those he left behind. Following his marriage to Susan, Merrick has been placed in charge of the States Police and has suddenly met his death, apparently from a riding accident. Perron's letters to Sarah have remained unanswered and she seems rather detached

The Layton family and friends board a train at Mirat for the fateful journey to Ranpur.

when they meet again, deeply involved with Ahmed Kasim in managing the Nawab's household. Nigel Rowan is dashing off on political business but lends Perron the use of his bungalow. No one is anxious to discuss how Merrick died.

In the compound Perron meets young Edward, Susan's little son, who takes him to his parents' bungalow nearby. He shows Perron a picture which his step-father gave him – 'The Jewel in the Crown'. Here Perron also meets Susan, kneeling beside a trunkful of Merrick's possessions and clearly distracted by his death. She talks obsssessively about her husband – wondering what happened to his metal arm and to the Pathan clothes he used for spying. 'Ronnie was afraid of nothing. I depended on him, Mr Perron, you see.'

Sarah takes Perron into the country to watch Ahmed hawking – a sport which is now his passion. At the palace he is welcomed by Count Bronowsky and together they discuss the critical decision facing the Nawab – political independence for his small state or integration with the forthcoming Indian Union territory around it. Communal violence threatens Mirat, ruled by a Muslim prince but largely Hindu. It seems that Indian independence may release a Pandora's Box filled with troubles that British rule has kept locked away.

When Rowan returns late that night he brings the news that he has at last persuaded the Nawab to accede his state to India. Perron intends to leave Mirat with the Laytons in two days' time and now he probes Rowan to tell him the truth about Merrick's death. Rowan reveals that Merrick was murdered – strangled in his bed. 'Everything's properly recorded, but a murdered Englishman at this time is the last thing anybody wants.' Hari Kumar is not a suspect. Since his release from prison he has been living quietly in Ranpur giving English lessons and – as Perron now discovers – writing occasional pieces for the local press. One of these evokes an image of Hari as he walks away under the trees – recalling memories under the shade of different trees in another place – 'dreams never fulfilled, never to be fulfilled . . .' Perron has returned to an India which hovers uneasily between dream and nightmare.

ABOVE
The camera is secured to the steam engine to film the train's approach towards the cow tethered to the line.

RIGHT
A sacred cow is tethered to the railway line by armed men intent on attacking the Mirat–Ranpur train.

OPPOSITE
Bandits wait to attack the Mirat–Ranpur train in a sequence filmed at Dubari, near Udaipur.

EPISODE FOURTEEN — *A Division of the Spoils*

On the eve of his departure from Mirat, Perron dines with Bronowsky. There is tension in the city as India prepares for the break with Pakistan; Hindus and Muslims are burning one another's shops. Bronowsky describes to Perron the horror surrounding Merrick's death – probably brought about through his homosexual relations with a servant-boy – a ritual killing in a blood-soaked room, the word 'Bibighar' scrawled across his mirror. 'I believe he wanted it, waited for his death. What was destroyed was the belief in his racial superiority.'

Next day Bronowsky and Rowan are on the platform to say goodbye. Perron is travelling to Ranpur with Ahmed to interview his father 'MAK' Kasim, the leading Muslim politician. Aunt Fenny accompanies Sarah, Susan and little Edward, who have been joined by two typical members of the departing Raj, the Peabodys. The journey in the crowded first-class compartment begins pleasantly enough, although the Peabodys resent the presence of Ahmed and little Edward's ayah. Suddenly the train stops on an empty plain. Susan clutches the box which contains Merrick's ashes. 'Probably a cow on the line.' Ahmed looks out of a window – then swiftly begins to pull down the blinds as there are distant sounds of breaking glass, shouting and screaming. A pounding on the door follows with cries for Ahmed Kasim. Ahmed says: 'It seems to be me they want' – then jumps from the compartment. After a time, the train begins to pull away in terrible silence.

The full horror of what has happened is revealed in Premanagar station. Muslim men, women and children have been butchered in their carriages. Sarah and Perron do what they can, but each is overwhelmed by a sense of guilt and futility. 'Ahmed and I weren't in love,' Sarah tells him, 'but we loved one another. I'm sure he smiled just before he went . . . Nothing that we could do. Like Daphne Manners. Like Hari Kumar. After three hundred years of India, we've made this whole damned bloody senseless mess.' Perron is to return to Mirat to break the news to the palace. Carrying Ahmed's small canvas bag he turns back for a last look at Sarah before he goes.

Just before his Dakota takes off from India, Perron makes a sudden decision to seek out Hari Kumar at the address which Rowan has given him. But when he reaches the tenement in a crowded Indian street, he finds that Hari is not at home. Perron can only leave his card with the boy who has helped him find his way – not knowing whether his action will have done harm or good in Hari's solitary life. He goes – leaving the mystery of Hari Kumar and India's tangled history behind him.

Guy Perron surveys the scene of carnage at Premanagar Station after the savage attack on his train from Mirat.

⚜4⚜

The Last Days of the Raj

A PERSONAL VIEW

by JAMES CAMERON

In the history of man's dominion over man, or nation over nation, the British Empire was – using the word exactly – unique. Other empires have come, and endured, and disappeared; for several thousand years the entire framework of what was defined as civilization was dominated by this or that alien authority – Babylonian, Roman, Greek, Byzantine, Islamic, each in succession strutting its fading hours until it collapsed, or decayed, or wasted away, leaving its little mark in language or custom or artefact, to be absorbed or rejected by its successors.

The British Empire was one of many. But it was the most memorable, the most famous, the most varied, at the same time the most arrogant and the most domestic, paradoxically the most bitter and most affectionate, succeeding at the end in welding wholly incompatible societies into a political pastiche that never truly became coherent, and yet cohered. Even when it was all over the component parts that had argued and fought so long and hard to be free clung inexplicably to a nostalgic past and turned an empire into a Commonwealth. What had started off in Elizabethan grandeur came to an end in Cromwellian – or rather Crippsian – compromise.

And of this eccentric, inexplicable, ad hoc, multicoloured congeries of societies the historically greatest in every way was the only one of which Victoria was 'Empress' – India, the Raj, the Jewel in the Crown.

The 'Raj' simply means – or meant – the 'Rule'. English nouns, especially when adapted from other tongues, are capable of a great variety of subtle interpretations: 'Raj' went into the Anglo-Indian vocabulary for about two centuries as meaning not so much suzerainty, or boss-dom, or government, but as simply an accepted and possibly God-given state of affairs that had long ago ordained that the British should rule and dominate India. That it should have been thus ordained that a comparative handful of paleface Anglo-Saxons should assume the political, military, and even moral mastery of several hundred million brown heathens was a fact of life, an act of God, a circumstance of grace. The British Raj in India not only gave thanks, occasionally, to the Almighty for according Britain the res-

67

Highnesses and lownesses The classic picture from the Raj at the turn of the century: two live noblemen with their feet on two dead Indians. Lord Curzon in the exotic European dress and the Maharajah of Gwalior, in native attire, have clearly had a good day. It might be thought less good by the tigers. But this was 1900, when Rulers and Viceroys were protected species.

ponsibility of looking after India for India's spiritual sake and HMG's financial advantage, but required India to do the same.

And indeed India did, for a long long time. The British presence made many Indians very rich, whilst allowing millions more to starve to death. The rich did their thing ostentatiously and with the stagecraft of which the Victorians approved; the poor died quietly and alone.

It was a benevolent Raj, a cruel Raj, above all an ignorant and indifferent Raj. On the whole, it has been argued, it did more good than harm. It worked according to the mores of the time. The complicated moralities of imperialism are now academic, now that imperialism has withered away. The Indian Empire was in its day something the world had never known before, and certainly will never know again.

We enter the story in its twilight. Or not quite: Paul Scott's India is only just sensing the setting of the sun, still refusing to look it in the eye.

This was not, as much of the world believed at the time, through imperial possessiveness. The Indian Empire had for several generations been no special matter of pride: it was just a fact of life. The British had been established there so long that the middling level of the ruling-class India was emotionally, if not in fact, a sort of suburb – either of Wimbledon, among the Sahibs, or something like Oldham among the trading box-wallahs of Bengal. Inevitably they despised each other far more than they did the Indians, whose social mysteries went on as a sort of background, both inexplicable and irrelevant. For them the real India was rather like the solar system, a surrounding something that had always been and for ever would be accepted, and even studied, but which could hardly be changed. At home the majority of middle- and working-class British rarely gave the place a thought, except as an occasional lush setting for romantic movies. It was there; it was ours; we kept an Army there for reasons never wholly explained. India was British as, doubtless, the moon was British; when was it otherwise?

Yet, very evidently, it was changing, and this disagreeable fact had to be taken account of. Just as the European-German war was on the English doorstep, so the Japanese war was approaching ever nearer to inviolable India. At this very moment the unspeakable Japanese had defeated the British Army in Burma, which was just round the corner as it were; the even more despicable Hitler was having his own way on the Continent of Europe. Clearly the managers of history – the Almighty, or whoever had taken over Fate – had got his cues mixed up, and the script of destiny was going wrong.

Moreover, in inviolable India the British were now continually reminded that their personal opponent was no longer just outside the gates but within them. The mild, pacific, and faintly ridiculous figure of Mahatma Gandhi was seeking every advantage from the discomfiture of the British, who had for so long been an oppressive but apparently immovable ruler but who now, with their military backs against the wall, could possibly turn nasty.

Gandhi's innovation, with his emphasis on *Swaraj* – self-rule – and *swadeshi* – Indian-made goods, was that he took politics to the people. He shifted the struggle from the middle class to the masses. By the time of the 'Raj Quartet' Gandhism was a fact of life, taken far more seriously in London and Viceregal Lodge than in the British business or military circles. Gandhi in his loin-cloth and shawl and strange little wizened spectacled appearance, could be seen by the minor sahibs as faintly absurd, and this was the easy way of dismissing him. After all, Winston Churchill had called him 'a naked fakir', and Churchill should know.

The British Empire, of course, was only the last of a long line of alien dominations. It seemed that India, enormous and populous as it was, was decreed by some sort of fate, or *dharma*, to be for ever the fief or outpost of other powers. It had always had alien masters. It has been endlessly argued – and equally endlessly denied – that there has always been something in the Hindu (or even pre-Hindu) character that was inevitably subservient, that actually accepted a secondary role. All Indian patriots would denounce this as a cruel heresy, and to be sure the kind of Indians who would denounce this would be right; otherwise there would have been no Tipu Sahib, and no Mahatma Gandhi, no Indian Mutiny and no Subhas Bose, no visionaries or rebels. Nevertheless had the theory not been roughly true, there would have been no need of them, either.

It was not just a strange country into which Europe had strayed: it was a continent of such enormous complication – physical, geographical, sociological – that it is fair to say it was not, nor could be, called a 'country' at all until the British came and unified it, and this took centuries. Even as recently as the start of this one, the official records defined it as: twelve provinces under direct British administration, and scores of feudatory states and principalities, self-ruling but acknowledging the paramountcy of the British Crown. Independence simplified much of that, but India has always been a continent rather than a nation – a million and a half square miles of it; the highest snowy mountains in the world and the flattest, hottest plains; fourteen different official languages and several hundred dialects. It became a 'nation' politically and emotionally but in no other way.

Everything Indian – society, behaviour, politics – is informed and dominated by religion. It is inescapable, and no serious record can dodge it. Defining it is a different matter.

We know now that long ago the Aryan invaders from central Asia devised a polytheistic religious arrangement in the Rig-Veda hymns that had evidence of a philosophical and political coherence. They simplified the unbearably complicated

Rails and mountains Perhaps the main thing for which modern India can thank Edwardian England—and generously does—is one of the longest and most complicated railway systems in the world. The railways, with their thousands of miles, unite the vast distances of India as nothing else could do, or ever did. Especially in the north, railway engineering has opened up countryside that could never otherwise be seen.

Here is the Halkar State Railway, on the North-West Frontier, an astonishing feat of landscape engineering nearly ninety years ago, and still going strong.

And below, the building of the East Bengal Railway, spanning the broad rivers with their enormous bridges.

To the hills The other great Anglo-Saxon contribution to Indian civilization—or so they say—is the Hill Station, to which the Sahibs could retreat when the heat of the plains grew too intense even for civil servants. The Hill Stations were, and remain, gracious country estates in the Himalaya or the Nilgiri hills. They created the Indian word 'banglo', and transformed it into 'bungalow'.

All these are English summer establishments either in Simla, in the far north, or Ootacamund in the deep south—'their little bit of England in the sun'.

hierarchical system of almost innumerable 'castes' by rationalizing them down to four major divisions, which indeed endure more or less substantially to this day – the Brahmins, priests; the Kshatriyas, warriors; the Vaisyas, or Banias, merchants; and the Sudras, or peasants. Beyond these groupings remain the Out-castes, the so-called Untouchables whom Gandhi tried to redeem by re-naming them 'Harijan': Children of God.

This uniquely Hindu phenomenon, the most explicitly anti-democratic system in the world – since no man can change castes in his lifetime, after which he can, according to his behaviour, be re-incarnated either up or down – has always been opposed by progressive Indians, and indeed the founding fathers of Independent India strove vigorously to abolish it constitutionally. To this day caste has proved impossible to eradicate even among the enlightened. In the thousands of villages of India – still after three decades of freedom largely illiterate – it is markedly more entrenched than ever. This is yet one more of India's endless paradoxes. The

Back in 1930 the police could still arrest the Congress pickets with a kind of affectionate tolerance. They were not important—yet.

British overlords tried in a listless way to discourage it and, finding they could not, quietly came to terms with it. They had, after all, a pretty well-developed caste-system of their own.

It is important to remember that the British did not take over Indian rule from the Indians, but from the Muslims. As the British were the last Indian Imperialists, the Moguls were the first. The Moguls – or Mongols – were the great martial Muslims from Persia and Arabia, who strove to dominate the East. Their Indian Empire was founded in 1526 by Babur, a descendant of Tamerlane, and lasted two hundred years from its great centre in Delhi. Most of the famous and enduring monuments of India were Mohammedan palaces and mosques – best known, of course, the Taj Mahal. Their monotheistic faith was totally at odds with the multi-god Hinduism, a fact that is still, and will probably be for ever, a cause of conflict in a nation that is obliged to harbour them both, by the millions.

The Moguls controlled India, at least nominally, until the early eighteenth century, reaching their zenith a hundred years earlier under the famous Emperor Akbar. His dominion stretched from Bengal in the east to Godavari in the south. Kashmir, Sind and Baluchistan were annexed; the Rajput princes were his tributaries. But by 1700 the Moguls were already moribund. The British were able to destroy them within ten years.

One is driven to believe that a great deal of imperishable history is brought about by chance. That a businesslike commercial company formed in the City of London for trading with 'the Indies' – which at that time meant almost anything east of Suez – came to establish itself as the dominant ruling and even military power in an enormous continent many thousands of miles across the world seems fanciful today. Yet this founding of the East India Company in 1600 under the patronage of the Lord Mayor of London and Queen Elizabeth I, in that order, is best and most reasonably described by a thoughtful and experienced Indian, product of Allahabad, Balliol and the Temple – B. K. Nehru, for five years in the 1950s High Commissioner in London:

It was proof that nature abhors a vacuum, which was filled by the representatives of a small and distant country because they were superior to the Indians of the day in organization, discipline, unity, and fire-power. Indian society of the time was tradition-bound and decadent, having lost all its resilience to meet new situations it was in no position to resist.

Coming from a Brit. or a Sahib this would sound patronizing, if not contemptuous, but it is objectively true. The notion of 'territorial nationalism' did not even exist in India. Any loyalty there was belonged first to families, then to individual princes or dynasties. The British, in short, were not hostile aliens; they were just the people of one more prince involved in one more interminable civil war.

The only explanation of the endurance of British rule in India is that it was, for years, never opposed. Had the Indians not co-operated, it would never have been possible for such a tiny British presence to dominate such a vast ocean of strangers. And the moment this popular co-operation became clearly reluctant and unwilling, British authority came to an end.

Until not long ago it was correct and acceptable to denounce the British – i.e. the Company's – rule in India as simple commercial brigandage and exploitation, which to some degree it was. Yet, however mercenary its motives, it must be said for the unlovable British that they imposed order and a sort of unity, and if its standards were sometimes pretty questionable they were higher than the existing ones. Even though the Company existed by wielding military power without political responsibility, even though it was shamelessly venal and profiteering, even though Clive and his company of 'Nabobs', as they were called, prospered on enormous bribery – nevertheless the awful truth is that not only was the Company the strongest and most efficient government India had known, it was paradoxically also the most enlightened. Without these selfish graceful crooks there might never have been a United India at all.

Nevertheless, in a hard world, India was the creation of businessmen. When

'John Company' disappeared, and Queen Victoria moved in as managing director, she proclaimed to the 'Princes, Chiefs, and Peoples of India' that Empire had taken over where Company left off, but that the policy of the charter would remain intact. The only change was that the President of Directors was replaced by a Secretary of State.

By the successful end of the First World War, the British Empire began to present a huge complication of human and political problems that England was frankly not equipped to handle. The *hope* for Indian independence was tirelessly expressed (indeed the 1919 Government of India Act offered Indians 'an association with administration', that is to say responsible government in India as part of the British Empire); the *fact* was burked. The days of John Company had often been criticized for profiteering and patronage and corruption. But now India was a part of the Crown – indeed its Jewel – and moreover the biggest foreign market any country had ever been able to control. And – *of course* – the Indians rejoiced in the benefits of British rule – beneficent, uncorrupt, non-capricious, without temptation or religious hate. It was a consoling idea.

It mattered very little to anyone outside India that an ancient village economy was destroyed by a deluge of machine-made cotton goods from Lancashire, that millions of Indian spinners and weavers were dispossessed and ruined. Indians were obliged to pay for the costs of their own subjugation. Even the military operations to suppress the Indian Mutiny were charged to the Indian taxpayer. It was a bizarre fact of Imperial ingenuity that the British not only conquered India with mainly Indian soldiers but actually obliged the Indians to pay for this paradoxical privilege.

The subsequent story of the growth of the increasingly determined Indian Nationalism is not a long one, but complicated. Too often recorded, too readily

In conference For some reason they called this the Round Table. It was in St James's Palace, 1931—one of so many Round Table Conferences interminably to debate the future of India. In the chair is Lord Sankey: on his left M. K. Gandhi and Pandit Malariya; on his right Lord Peel and Sir Samuel Hoare.

forgotten. Like everything in India a simple end was bedevilled by a lunatic conflict of means: India wanted to be free, Britain wanted India to be free – but in good time, in proper season, with no trouble or snags. Inevitably there arose nothing but snags, and by no means only on one side.

Indian historians record so many 'turning-points' in the British relationships that the cause of Independence in retrospect resembles any of the major and more confusing Indian traffic roundabouts. One of the most significant, however, came in 1909, in what became known as the Morley-Minto plan. Morley was the Secretary of State, Minto the Governor-General. By that time terrorism in Bengal had become widespread. The urgent revolutionary groups were increasingly critical of Congress moderation. The British Liberal cabinet became convinced that unless something very quickly happened things would fall to bits. The Liberal British Government openly favoured reform: the Indian political grievances were on the whole substantial and urgently needed to be put right – but again, of course, with caution and moderation. The Morley-Minto team were working with a Government that just could not *decide* anything. They had to propose not a clear-cut plan, but a set of compromise expedients: the age-old story of the Raj.

In a word, the violent men had to be crushed. At the same time the Moderates had to be appeased. Indian members would be admitted to the Secretary of State's Council in London. A rather celebrated Indian lawyer, who by and by became Lord Sinha, joined the Governor-General's Executive Council.

This was not nearly good enough for the Indian National Congress. It wanted more Indians on the legislative council, a heavy development of the elective principle. This looked a bit thick even for the liberal Morley. Next thing these people would demand was British-type constitutional government. Indians could be allowed to participate, to counsel, but not, surely, to control. However, the Morley-Minto reforms allowed the Indian legislative councils to pass resolutions – they even conceded that its members might be elected, but not by territorial constituencies, as in Britain, but by what were called Special Interests.

At this point, as usual, in came the Muslim League. It had first met in 1906, in Dacca – which is now in Bangladesh – and at this time was led by the Aga Khan,

74

an enormous landowner in Bombay. Why, they protested, by this scheme the Muslims would be only half-represented. The British – who throughout their Imperial history had always listened more sympathetically to forceful Islam than to the cultivated heathen, like Hindus and Jews – conceded to the Muslims a separate self-voting electorate, based not on their numbers but on their importance.

This – inevitably and naturally – was 'divide and rule'. From then on the Muslims of India began to think and act as Muslims, not Indians. Whether this was guile or simplicity is argued to this day, but whatever it was, half a century later it led to the bisection of India and the amputation of Pakistan, and the Lords Morley and Minto were to blame. If, indeed, blame is the word.

From the time of the 'Morley-Minto reforms' it was obvious that a Liberal England accepted the inevitability of a dignified and self-sufficient India; if only both Britain and India could agree on what that was. Economically both sides became dependent on each other, industry and commerce grew, many people in both communities became very rich, and the enormous Indian peasant majority became poorer and poorer. The very first census in 1872 showed 206 millions; in 1911 it was 315 millions. (Today it is a wholly speculative 700 millions, and growing at a rate of about ten a minute, a calculation almost incomprehensible outside Asia, and deeply frightening.)

Something had to give.

One more great oddity in a country of inconsistencies is that the Indian National Congress – the organization that dominated anti-colonial Indian politics from their beginning – was created by an Englishman: Allan Octavian Hume – an English public-school product who joined the Bengal Civil Service (as it was called then) in 1849. He had, for such a man, an eccentric idealism. He started an organization to further the patriotic ambitions of literate Indians. This in fact became, in 1885, Congress itself, with one W. C. Bonnerji, a former Civil Servant, its first President. Its initial delegates were seventy-six – mainly Hindu, with a

A

F

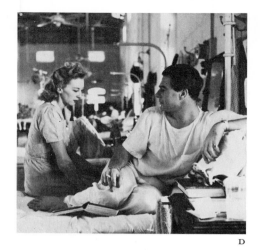

D

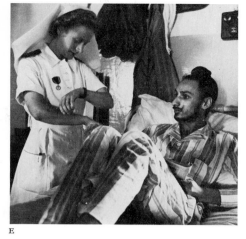

E

B

EUROPEAN LADIES

East is East and West is West and ever the twain did meet— at least at the right level, which meant between the Raj and the Rich.

(A) India gave us polo. (In revenge we gave them cricket.) In the 1930s polo meant young grandees like the Crown Prince of Patiala, the senior State of the bearded Sikhs. (B) Elsewhere the sides kept to themselves, and especially the women. On social occasions the ladies knew their place, and 'European Ladies' more than most.

(C) The Club in the brave days was even more exclusive and monastic; the exclusion of Indians other than servants was among the most bitter resentments of the time, and the Peshawar Club was an archetype.

In the wartime European hospitals (D, E: photos by Cecil Beaton) there was no dilemma— as there was no dilemma (F) in the urban ghettoes of the Hindu Untouchables, the total basement of the Hindu caste-system. The humane Gandhi compassionately renamed them 'Harijan'—the Elect of God. But they still lived like this, and still do.

(G) A snake-charmer at Puri, 1942.

G

C

Best of foes Two dominant Indian patriots took totally opposite lines on Independence: Vallabhabhai Patel the traditionalist, and Subhas Chandra Bose the revolutionary. Patel (pictured right) returned from the Middle Temple to become vigorous in Gandhi's Indian National Congress. He was to become the first Deputy Prime Minister under Jawaharlal Nehru and all his life was the staunchest of conservatives.

Subhas Bose, on the other hand, took the road of blood and fire. He had been Congress President, but with the coming of the war he decided that Japan offered more hope to India than Britain did and defected to the enemy, never to be officially encountered again. He was traced to Germany, where he sought the aid of Hitler, and again to Japan, where he undertook the formation of an Indian National Army from among the great numbers of Indian Army prisoners-of-war in order to fight on the Japanese side. The effort came to little, though later there were several War Crimes trials of defecting Indians.

Bose himself appears to have vanished. He was reported from time to time in Axis centres, but after 1945 he was never seen. He is thought to have been killed in a Japanese air-crash, but it was never established how or where he died.

This is thought to be the last picture ever taken of the two strange colleagues who worked for the same end in such very different ways.

few Parsis and Jains (small but influential minorities) – lawyers, teachers, journalists, many of them Western-educated. Hume had hopes that one day – one day – it would develop into an Indian Parliament, which, of course, it finally did, though thirty years too late for him to see it.

The first Indian National Congress of 1885 prudently stressed loyalty to Britain. The next, in the following year, had 440 delegates, and was more patriotic. At the beginning the movement was basically Hindu. The Muslims worked through the Muslim League Association. (It was not until 1916 that both bodies combined in a declaration for Indian Home Rule. From then on Congress came to be regarded as the central nationalist movement in the subcontinent.)

Under the leadership of M. K. Gandhi – to whom we shall shortly and inescapably return – Congress absorbed virtually all enlightened nationalist minds, from moderate to extreme. It was often sharply divided, on philosophical and practical grounds, but throughout all its vicissitudes it remained – indeed until recently – the one organization able to make the country cohere and stimulate mass movements. The readiness – almost sometimes the eagerness – of its leaders to risk and sometimes suffer imprisonment had an enormous effect. Only after Independence did its divisions cause it to split, when Mrs Indira Gandhi's idiosyncratic rule became divisive – but there, as Kipling so often said, is another story.

It is a confusing necessity to explain that it is by the sheerest chance that the present Prime Minister of India and its great Founding Father share the same name. They are related in no way. 'Gandhi' is not an uncommon Indian name: it means 'grocer'. To the patrician Kashmiri Brahmin lady who leads the nation now there must be mixed feelings about sharing the name of a humble Bania-caste lawyer from the Kathiawar peninsula, but the huge public-relations advantages must far outweigh the embarrassment.

Mrs Indira Gandhi is the only daughter of the late and great Jawaharlal Nehru, India's first Prime Minister. In 1941 Indira Nehru married Feroze Gandhi, who died not long ago (and who was, incidentally, a Parsi), but after Independence in 1947 she devoted her life to acting as companion and hostess for her widowed father. Combining as she does the two most historically resounding names in the Congress canon she was celebrated without even trying. Which is not to say that she has not greatly tried, to the extent of suffering imprisonment herself in 1941,

thus maintaining the patriotic tradition of her father, mother and grandfather.

The real Gandhi is something else again.

In *The Story of My Experiments with Truth* Mohandas Karamchand Gandhi long ago defined once and for all time the character and motivation of his Indian struggle – though 'defined' is hardly the exact word for Gandhi's mysterious mixture of the spiritual and the practical, the ineffable and the down-to-earth, the compassionate and the ruthless, the holy and the cunning. By and by he came to be known only as the 'Mahatma', or Great Soul. The title was conferred on him spontaneously by the whole nation; no definition of a human being has ever been so complete and total. It was characteristic of this unique little man – probably the most influential human leader who ever existed – that he disclaimed the honorific, but never for a moment rejected it.

Gandhiji – the 'ji' is an untranslatable suffix implying simultaneous respect and affection – was born in 1869 at Porbander on the coast of the Arabian Sea. He was of the middling Bania – or merchant – caste, neither high nor low; it made no difference to a man for ever dedicated to the abolition of all the arbitrary hierarchies of caste, and creed, and colour. He broke all the rules, which is how he became historically immortal. He was a rather ugly, graceless little man. Yet his name became almost divine on the one hand and derided on the other. This even among Indians, today, who owe whatever dignity and nationhood they have to this ostentatiously modest and gently ironclad little Gujerati lawyer who took on the might of the British Raj and – to begin with alone – reduced it to nothing, and in his lifetime.

The British mocked him, rejected him, imprisoned him, and eventually, as the British always do, saluted him and enshrined him. He was either the greatest patriot in the world, or its greatest con-man.

The first Hindu rule Gandhi broke was to go abroad.

In 1888 Gandhi went to England; he studied in University College, London, and was called to the Bar at the Inner Temple. All manner of fanciful tales are

India: The Last Chance This became a famous and even historic photograph: one of the seminal moments in the growth to independence. February 1947, in the Constituent Assembly in New Delhi: Pandit Jawaharlal Nehru moves to a crowded House the resolution for an Independent Sovereign Republic.

told about this simple Hindu's problems with formal European clothes and carnivorous English food. Whatever those deep social problems, he surmounted them – but never, to be sure, forgot them. He returned to India, qualified, in 1891, and began practice at the Supreme Court of Bombay.

Soon afterwards business took him – momentously as it turned out – to South Africa. What he found there decided him to remain, to work for the cause of the many Indian immigrants, who were manifestly, racially, oppressed even then. It was in South Africa that he devised what was to become his life's gospel – *satyagraha*, or 'non-violent non-cooperation', which was to become the dominant theme of his life's endeavour.

At the beginning of the First World War Gandhi returned to India, his destiny prepared. It was to grow hugely in scope and importance, but its genesis was modest. He founded an *ashram,* a place of retreat where could be led a life of *ahimsa:* total respect for all life, truth, celibacy, simplicity. It ran counter to everything the world had up to then come to know as Politics. Indeed in later years both British and Indians came to find a resemblance between the political methodologies of M. K. Gandhi and Jesus Christ; it was not an altogether fanciful analogy.

In the First World War Gandhi's actions were – as so often – ambivalent. When it began he went to London to organize an Indian ambulance corps, and professed his support for the British cause, which he held to be marginally better than the Kaiser's.

Back in India his *satyagraha* policy exasperated the British but did not unduly dismay them even though it did not always follow the peaceful course laid down by Gandhi's ethics. 'Civil Disobedience' became the slogan. Gandhi formally disapproved, but could not prevent it.

Despite India's co-operation in the First World War, in India itself social discrimination and inequalities remained. The Indians were not cowed but uneasy; the British responded by the Defence of India Act and the Rowlatt Act. These were tantamount to detention without trial. Fear prevailed on both sides. Gandhi became wholly alienated. By 1922 thirty thousand Indians were in jail.

Gandhi had assumed the mantle of Congress leader. He declared a *hartal* (a peculiarly Indian form of General Strike, by which everything was brought to a standstill – factories, schools, bazaars). In the Punjab, an incident took place in which a couple of English were killed. To 'teach the natives a lesson' martial law was declared and curfew was imposed at Amritsar by General Dyer.

On 13 April 1919 a defiant but peaceful crowd gathered to protest in an open square in Amritsar. Without warning, the troops opened fire on a crowd defenceless and trapped. In a few minutes nearly four hundred were dead and two thousand wounded. Even medical assistance was stopped. Not satisfied with this extraordinary show of brutality General Dyer passed the 'crawling order', by which Indians were obliged to crawl on their stomachs to reach their homes.

Liberal opinion in Britain was outraged, and demanded the return of General Dyer, but public opinion was so much in his favour amongst the British in India and conservatives at home that £26,000 was collected for his benefit, and doubtless he died content.

Amritsar was the great and symbolic punctuation-mark in India-British relations. A shock-wave went through the entire country, and for the first time bitterness began. M. K. Gandhi never truly trusted the Raj again.

But his importance grew – as a politician and agitator, and even more so as a prophet in revolt against all the ideas of modernism, machinery, science, all forms of state control and violence. To the Indian masses he was the nearest human thing to a saint. The British never came to understand the contrast between the wise, simple and brave social reformer and the exasperating hair-splitting demagogue, who preached poverty and relied on immensely rich industrialists to support him.

Gandhi in fact called off the Civil Disobedience. But in 1922 he was arrested and tried at Ahmedabad and sentenced to six years in prison for preaching disaffection. He accepted the sentence gracefully – almost, some said, gratefully. After two years he was released, and decided to renounce politics, travelling round the villages of India, fighting Untouchability and promoting handweaving and spinning. By this time most of rural India saw him as a sort of reincarnation of God.

However, Gandhi could not long be kept from worldly politics. In the late 1920s he was once again elected President of Congress – he declined it, leaving it to his distinguished lieutenant Motilal Nehru, who was quickly succeeded by his even more celebrated son, Jawaharlal Nehru.

In 1930 came Gandhi's famous Salt March to the sea, publicly to violate the Government salt monopoly by distilling salt from sea water on the shore. He was sentenced to be kept in jail near Poona 'during the Government's pleasure'. It was soon fulfilled: the next year Gandhi was released to attend the famous Round Table Conference in London.

From then on the story of Mahatma Gandhi is of recurrent campaigns, arrests, imprisonments, and releases. Tired of this, in 1935 he announced he was abandoning politics and retiring to his *ashram* in Wardha. It was a hopeless plan. By now he was so wholly identified with the Nationalist movement and had so captured the heart of India as a human saint, that retreat was impossible. India and Gandhi – neither could exist without the other.

The Second World War presented India with a distressful dilemma. Gandhi accepted that Hitler was the aggressor, and that Britain could morally ask India's support. But, said Gandhi, that support could come only from a Free India, and his demand for 'complete independence' became more insistent. The British equivocated. It seemed evident that the Administration was actively promoting discord between Hindus and Muslims, on the long-established divide-and-rule principle.

In the summer of 1942 Gandhi lost his temper and demanded an immediate British withdrawal from India.

The British reaction was summary: to imprison the whole Congress leadership. It was a vain and silly gesture; two years later Gandhi and all his disciples were released, so that the interminable question of Independence could once more be renewed. By that time Gandhi had in fact formally withdrawn from active membership of Congress. But of course he continued to dominate the Party from without.

Gandhi was envisaged by his disciples as a mystic; by his opponents as a tiresome agitator and ambitious hypocrite. Characteristically he was neither, and both. His total originality was simultaneously to involve the manifold aspects of Hinduism in all other creeds, dramatizing the whole gesture by, firstly, his own example, and then by a torrent of essays, articles, and speeches. He was far from unaware of the power of personal theatre – the loin-cloth, the spinning-wheel, the days of silence, the famous Fasts: they all made great sense to a largely illiterate following. He did not call protest meetings: he called a *hartal,* a religious strike. He went enthusiastically to prison, in order that he could emerge in triumph. It was metaphysical politics that totally confounded the British Raj, as Gandhi knew all the time that it must do.

Five major events marked this period: the Stafford Cripps mission of 1942; the Quit India movement of the same time; the Simla Conference of 1945; the Cabinet Mission of the following year; finally the Mountbatten Partition Plan of 1947. Historians have rightly said that the whole enormous episode was shaped by the personalities of twelve individuals. Seven were on the British side – Churchill, Amery, Cripps, Attlee, Linlithgow, Wavell, and Mountbatten, and five on the Indian side – M. K. Gandhi, Mohammed Ali Jinnah, Maulana Azad, Jawaharlal Nehru, and Valabhbhai Patel. The Paul Scott period was dominated by this group as India had never been dominated before.

The Cripps Mission of 1942 was of course climactic: for the first time it was

The rebel Subhas Chandra Bose, the self-exiled Indian Nationalist, arriving in Singapore in 1943 to cast in his lot with the Japanese.

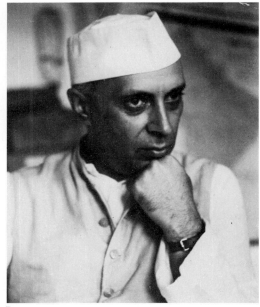

A   B

The President of the Muslim League, Mohammed Ali Jinnah —for once, unusually, in Indian dress (A) addressing the League in Delhi, while his Congress counterpart Jawaharlal Nehru (B) looks and listens.

The British Cabinet Mission (C), newly arrived to negotiate the excruciatingly difficult terms of Independence—Lord Pethick-Lawrence, A. V. Alexander and Sir Stafford Cripps—confer with the President of Congress, Maulana Kalam Azad, bearded, with his interpreter, the Congressman Asaf Ali.

suggested that the Indians should be given the right to frame their own Constitution, and the Muslim majority provinces allowed to opt out of the Indian Union altogether and constitute themselves into independent sovereign states. This was an immensely significant move and indeed changed Asian history and geography, since it advanced the idea of Pakistan when even Mohammed Ali Jinnah and his Muslim League hardly took it seriously.

By hindsight it is evident that this was the basic idea of a now almost-forgotten man, Leo Amery, then Secretary of State for India. Amery was a very pragmatic and somewhat parochial English politician, of whom English historians have said that his one foray into speculative thinking was to argue that what India needed was an increasing infusion of Nordic-type blood. Thus Muslim Independence would simultaneously punish Congress for being recalcitrant and bloody-minded,

C

and pat Jinnah's Muslims on the back for being so decently co-operative with the British.

The then Viceroy, Linlithgow, argued that even if Congress could be persuaded to accept the plan it would finish the Empire. Churchill, who denied the right of Indian Independence to his dying day, also believed that Congress would turn Partition down flat.

As for Stafford Cripps, the well-intentioned Christian innocent: he never realized that his Mission to India was intended by Churchill from the beginning to fail. Instead he worked desperately to make it succeed, promising indeed far more liberalities than the British Cabinet would have conceded.

We now know, from study of the documents of the time, that in 1942 Gandhi was convinced that the Japanese were going to win the war, that the British would retreat from India as they had fled from Burma and Malaya, and that the

D

E

A face from the past: Brigadier General R. E. Dyer, British commander at the time of the notorious Amritsar Massacre in 1919 (D).

And another (E): King George V and Queen Mary on their famous visit to India in 1911, in full array at the Delhi Durbar.

With Independence still a long way off, in 1931, M. K. Gandhi calls at Number 10 Downing Street to confer with Ramsay MacDonald (F).

With Independence approaching fast, the Indian leaders come to London for talks with the Government (G). From left to right: the Muslim leader Mr Jinnah, the Sikh leader Sardar Baldev Singh, Lord Pethick-Lawrence, Secretary of State for India, Pandit Jawaharlal Nehru, and V. K. Krishna Menon.

F

G

Japanese would not bother to attack India. The British, he argued, were now used to abandoning their colonies, and could be persuaded to leave India in good time. 'Leave India to God' he said, 'or if that is too much, leave her to anarchy.'

As ever, his apocalyptic language had a solid pragmatic base. Even as Stafford Cripps was negotiating with the Indian leaders Gandhi insisted that his non-violent creed obliged him to oppose India's involvement in the war. His especial fear was that if Congress accepted the Cripps offer – even with its clause about Muslim independence – India would be stuck on the losing side, and be saddled, however indirectly, with the victorious Japanese.

Right up to the summer of 1942, then, when the Quit India resolution was endorsed by Congress, Gandhi was working by guess and by God, still hoping that the Viceroy would call him in for negotiations. And then Linlithgow suddenly clamped down on Congress and arrested its leaders. The revolution, as it were, was on. The British hardened their attitude to Congress, which found itself in the political wilderness. Mr Jinnah was left unchallenged to strengthen his hold on the Muslim League, and the League to dominate Muslim politics in India.

Possibly history will consider that the major event of that period was the Simla Conference of 1945. This was in the final days of Winston Churchill's Prime Ministership. By then the Viceroy was Wavell – whose Viceroyalty, it seems now, was far more significant than that of his predecessor Linlithgow or of his more publicized successor Mountbatten. Wavell was in his way a tragic figure, a man of sensitivity driven into a job where that was the least helpful of qualifications. In the three and a half years from October 1943 to March 1947 he changed, as was said at the time, from a buoyant enthusiast to a melancholy defeatist.

Poor Wavell. Churchill had sacked him from his command in the Western Desert; he had been forgotten in Burma. He was militarily discredited, and his appointment as Viceroy was an expression of Churchill's simultaneous contempt for Wavell and for the Indians. What no one knew at the time was that Archibald Wavell was wholly aware of this, too. He knew very well how contemptuously Churchill considered the Viceregal job.

Most people more or less believed in the Churchill mythology, the image of the wartime paragon. It was a long time before the idolatry cracked enough to expose the rancour and prejudices and conceit and ill-tempered bitterness of the man. Wavell wrote: 'He hates India and everything to do with it, and as Leo Amery [the Secretary of State] said in a note he pushed across to me: "He knows as much of the Indian problem as George III did of the American colonies".'

Wavell was a discreet and even taciturn man in his public life, but candid in his diaries. Churchill was 'menacing and unpleasant'. He 'worked himself into a tirade against Congress and all its works' and said that only over his dead body would any approach be made to Gandhi. Even before Wavell left for India it was clear to him that the British Cabinet was dishonest in its expressed wish to make progress in India. 'You are being wafted to India,' said Amery, 'on a wave of hot air.'

Again: poor Wavell. He was briefed by the outgoing Viceroy, Linlithgow, to the effect that between the stupidity of the Indians and the dishonesty of the British the Raj would be obliged to stumble on for another thirty years. Within the year he 'found HMG's attitude to India negligent, hostile and contemptuous to a degree I had not anticipated . . . Winston sent me a peevish telegram to ask why Gandhi had not died yet!'

The Simla Conference did its best to foil the movement towards an independent Pakistan by forming a Coalition Government of Congress and the Muslim League on a parity basis. It was doomed from the start. Jinnah demanded for his Muslim League as many seats as Congress in the proposed provisional Government, though Muslims made up less than one-third of India's population. Wavell was advised by most of his governors to go ahead with forming a provisional Government without the Muslim League and, had he been given a free hand, Jinnah might have been persuaded to join a Coalition and history might have been wholly changed. Churchill and his Muslim sympathizers put a stop to that.

The enormous Lutyens boulevard in New Delhi was designed for great occasions, and saw many. This was the great Victory Day Parade in March 1946 marching towards Viceregal Lodge in the distance.

Home from home: the Raj at ease.

From all this hindsight Churchill's successor Clement Attlee emerges little better. Our great belief, or illusion, was that Indian Independence was the crowning glory of the post-war Labour Government in Britain, monument to the obstinately courageous statesmanship of Mr Attlee – that Mr Attlee sent this Cripps Mission to India somehow to persuade Congress and the Muslim League to come to terms in a united Central Government to which Britain could painlessly hand over.

Wavell's journals suggest this is a total fallacy. If any man had the credit for insisting that the only way out of a deadlock was a deadline, it was Wavell. Attlee not only never acknowledged this, but summarily fired Wavell for the suggestion – only to find his successor Mountbatten demanding the same thing, and refusing to take the Viceroy's job otherwise.

Gandhi told the Viceroy Wavell that 'sooner or later the British would have to come down on the side of Congress or the League'. Wavell tried valiantly to maintain a British impartiality, until it became evident that the new Labour Government was now opting for Congress.

It is now pretty clear that if Wavell had been allowed to treat freely with Jinnah, India might have entered Independence under a coalition, which would have changed history, and geography, and saved many thousand lives. But the idea of formalizing political parity in India between Hindus and Muslims was too much to swallow in the 1940s – especially by Viceroy Wavell, who so clearly shared the British Army's predilection in favour of Islam over idolaters. Wavell was a good and kind and reasonable man, but like all soldiers he saw Muslims as Christians-manqué, and Hindus as a 'pretty queer and alien lot'.

In the spring of 1946 Britain sent out the Three Cabineteers – Cripps, Alexander, and Pethick-Lawrence. (I was a camp-follower of that odd Anglo-Saxon ménage, of whom the brainy initiative clearly belonged to Stafford Cripps.) Wavell did not trust them an inch, believing that they came to India deeply committed to Congress – in which, as it turned out, he was on the whole right. Wavell, a frustrated poet and too sensitive a man to be a Civil Servant, had by now wholly lost faith in the unity of India and believed that a created Pakistan was the only answer to the apparently endless dilemma. By now one had come almost to sympathize with him; anything was better than this insoluble political-metaphysical dispute.

We now know that Wavell had rather oversimplified the situation. The Cabinet Mission was not all that committed to the Gandhi-Nehru Congress; they would have accepted that the Muslims were a minority, not a nation, and that the Pakistan creation was not a viable proposition. They did believe – at least to begin with – that a co-operative India was possible, if the Muslim-majority provinces were given autonomy, within an Indian Union. They could even be given the option of seceding – but after ten years. Paradoxically enough, this British plan was founded on a compromise notion devised by Maulana Azad, the leader of Congress who was himself a Muslim. It was far too reasonable to be accepted by Jinnah, Congress, or the British.

But all this was dreamland, depending on a mutual trust between the communities. It never stood a chance. The double suspicions of the Hindus of the Muslims, and vice versa, were by then entrenched to a point that in retrospect seems almost absurd.

Then out went Viceroy Wavell and in came the ultimate Viceroy, Mountbatten. Lord Mountbatten was an intelligent aristocrat, who somehow combined a scrupulous sense of duty with an effective appreciation of show-business vanity; he was a loyal patriot and an internationalist; he came to India on his own terms, knowing that his brief was effectively to pull the plug on the British Empire, and he accomplished it with authority and, indeed, grace. He, and his graceful and sociable Lady Mountbatten, achieved a relationship with the Congress leaders more intimate than any Viceregality before. It is said that Mountbatten's supreme ambition was to become the Joint Governor-General of both India and Pakistan, but naturally Jinnah would have none of this.

Lord Mountbatten, last of the Viceroys, will go down in history as a man flamboyant yet serious, vain yet dedicated, but essentially trivial. He despised Sir Stafford Cripps and derided his authority. 'You can't have leadership if you don't drink, don't smoke, don't eat, don't . . . .'

It has been recorded that Mountbatten's role was that of Official Receiver of the Raj. Clement Attlee had sent him to India with a mandate to obtain 'a unitary Government for British India and the Indian States if possible within the British Commonwealth'. Less than a month after arriving in India he came to the conclusion that this could never come about, because of Jinnah, and reconciled himself to Partition. Mountbatten could snub and overbear almost everyone, but he met his match with Mohammed Ali Jinnah and the Muslim League.

Jinnah was in his own strange way almost as bizarre a figure as his arch-opponent Gandhi. While Gandhi went about his affairs half-clad in a dhoti, M. A. Jinnah was

The inter-Indian rivalry in the final days of the British was symbolised in the intense personal conflict of Mohammed Ali Jinnah, of the Muslim League, and of course Mahatma Gandhi.

The two men had literally almost nothing in common, though both of them had been barristers in London. One strove to forget it, the other to perpetuate it. Mr Jinnah, obdurate apostle of Islam ('the man with a difficulty for every solution'), wore immaculate European dress; Gandhi's symbol was the homespun dhoti.

A

B

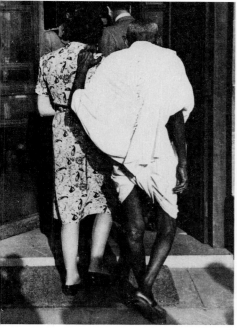

C   D

(A) Mr Jinnah, immaculate as ever, as a young law student at Lincoln's Inn in London.

(B) London's East Enders loved Mr Gandhi. In 1931 they mobbed him when he came to Canning Town for a meeting with another fan: Charlie Chaplin.

(C) Mr Gandhi leans on the shoulder of Lady Mountbatten as they enter Viceregal Lodge in New Delhi to confer with Viceroy Mountbatten.

(D) Mr M. A. Jinnah, the Muslim mastermind, with his sister and housekeeper Fatima. They lived in the house that had been built for Sir Edward Lutyens, creator of New Delhi.

(E) Mr Gandhi at Boulogne on his way to London for the Round Table Conference. The merry lady is Mrs Sarojini Naidu, famous poetess and wit and constant companion.

(F) Independence achieved, in 1947, Gandhi lost interest and hope; India he said, no longer heeded the imperative of peace. His granddaughters help him towards his 78th birthday, in 1947.

never publicly to be seen except in European clothes of a pedantic West Endish elegance that in its day could only be described as 'sharp'. From the beginning he had been inflexibly adamant that there could be no independence without partition. He never 'marched' or campaigned. He could not even speak Urdu. He was the total bureaucrat. Throughout the India of the Paul Scott era he was known as the man 'who had a difficulty for any solution'.

Mountbatten had demanded a wholly free hand, and got it, and used it. In 1947 he proclaimed that British power would be withdrawn not later than June 1948. It was a draconian gesture and startled the Indians, and even more the British, with its obvious certainty.

Since it was no longer a maybe-situation the inescapable had to be faced – Partition. On this Mr Jinnah wholly insisted. His Muslim League dominated the non-Hindu population. His two-nation plan was, like him, totally inflexible, and the League could block any Independence solution otherwise.

As Independence became inevitable, so came, though only to the north of India, civil war of the most appalling kind. Both communities exploded in vengeance

E   F

against each other, and there burst forth bitter and uncontrollable riots. Nothing so unnecessarily bloody had happened in India in the memory of anyone – Hindu, Muslim, or British. Jinnah declared an Action Day for August 1947. Desperate riots broke out in Calcutta, to the suffering of the Hindus. In Bihar the Hindus took their revenge, and it became worse in East Bengal and the United Provinces. Inevitably there were hideous excesses on both sides, breaking many hearts, in both shame and sorrow.

There was nothing the Raj could do except, quite summarily, opt out. It was the inescapable retreat, by shock treatment, and for once the British really meant business.

For Mahatma Gandhi it was the negation of his life's work. When the final triumph of Independence came in August 1947 it was empty. It was not one Free Nation; it was two; a partitioned Pakistan was his final sorrow. He did not even attend the Delhi celebration of his life's desire. There was bloodshed in Bengal, and where there was conflict the pacifist had to be.

He returned to Delhi, and made his familiar protest; he fasted.

He was persuaded by Jawaharlal Nehru to abandon the fast. By now he was pitifully weak, and despairing.

On 30 January 1948, at an evening prayer meeting at Birla House, he was approached by a stranger called Nathuran Godse. Godse was an extreme Hindu fanatic, obsessed with the illusion that Gandhi had betrayed the faith. He walked up to Gandhi, bowed and folded his hands in the reverent *namaste* gesture, produced a pistol and shot him dead.

And that was the senseless, ignoble end of Mahatma Gandhi, one of the world's great men.

Accepting that the whole Indian patriotic movement was dominated – at the time, and historically even now – by the tiny towering figure of Mahatma Gandhi, it could never have been fulfilled by him alone. The Congress organization was a consortium, a cast of highly varied characters all with special parts to play that were of equal meaning to the movement. They were united only in the goal, and broadly in the means of achieving it, but these tense individualists were not easily orchestrated into a unity. It is reasonable to say that no vast political movement was ever made so coherent by difference.

Its founding fathers are now dead, and the Party itself over recent years has suffered internecine feuds and divisions, but Congress to this day remains India, and India Congress, with Gandhi its patron saint.

Jawaharlal Nehru was Prime Minister of India from its Independence in 1947 until his death in 1964. He was the closest colleague of Gandhi, although they could hardly have differed more in background and temperament. Gandhi was an inspirational peasant; Nehru was an educated western-orientated patrician; he complemented the simplistic idealism of the Mahatma with the sophistication of a Harrow-and-Cambridge education. He would argue with Gandhi, but never oppose him. Through all the independence struggle he loyally followed the intuitive line of his leader, fulfilling it with his modern pragmatism.

Panditji – as he was called – could never claim to be an exceptional administrator. Yet after the murder of Gandhi few Indians would dispute that he was the voice of his nation. His belief in the principles of world-wide coexistence, guided by the tranquil philosophies of India, met with lifelong setbacks. Indeed his apparent condoning of Chinese intervention in Tibet lost him some friends in the liberal West, but during his lifetime he was virtually unchallenged, and his books – chiefly *Discovery of India* in 1945 – remain classics of both politics and literature. He died – diminished but deeply mourned – in 1964.

Today his daughter Indira rules in his stead. She has had her vicissitudes, and made her mistakes, but Indira inherits her father's quality of patriotism, with perhaps more worldly-wisdom to back it up.

Less than a year after Partition Mohammed Ali Jinnah, the architect and

founder of Pakistan (Land of the Pure), died suddenly, never tested, never proven, and therefore never diminished. He knew his political stature would be diminished in a free India and resolutely, stubbornly and finally successfully used the fear of religious sectarianism to create his new nation. He will be remembered with respect, even admiration, but never with affection. The country he created was officially a theocratic Muslim state, while the very first article of the Indian Constitution lays down – as Congress envisaged – that the new India would be free, non-ecumenical, open to all and every faith that upholds the law.

Congress was always proud to proclaim that one of its most distinguished leaders was not a Hindu. Maulana Azad was a distinguished Muslim, and an uncompromising believer in Indian Nationalism. But he refused on principle to join the Muslim League, and instead used his considerable influence on Congress to accept greater Muslim participation. As a political and religious radical he became a strong ally of Gandhi, and a similar temperament drew him to a close and lifelong friendship with Nehru.

A grandson of the Mufti of Medina, he had a traditional Muslim education, but from his youth he questioned any religion's claim to be the sole repository of Truth. While he had a high reputation among Muslim intelligentsia for his scholarship, he shocked conservative opinion with the radical views he expounded in his Urdu weekly.

Maulana Azad, the Muslim who was elected President of Congress, was a quiet and scholarly man. His life was of vast importance to the Freedom Movement, but somehow without flamboyance. His career followed the same pattern as other leaders, of frequent imprisonment from 1920 to 1945. He held office in the elections held by the British in 1937 and resigned in 1939. He supported Gandhi with the same loyalty as did Nehru.

His background and career bear a close resemblance to Paul Scott's Mir Kasim (MAK), and no doubt Scott used him as a model.

Azad became Minister of Education in 1947 and held that office till his death in 1958. He will be remembered as a quiet and thoughtful gentleman who rose above sectarianism and whose one ambition was the freedom and dignity of his country.

It probably never occurred to London that the Second World War could be the trigger for a militant Indian independence movement. Congress was genuinely anti-fascist. But the Viceroy, Lord Linlithgow, arrogantly declared India at war without consultation, and this, especially after the experience of the Great War, was wholly unacceptable.

The Indian National Army – Azad Hind Fauj – which believed in the values of violence, found its fulfilment in the Second World War. Its origins, however, had been much earlier. From 1900 onwards revolutionaries – wanted by the police, or lucky enough to escape from imprisonment in the British penal colony of the Andaman Islands – waited in the wings, in Tokyo and Bangkok. A few were well-to-do, most were brainy. All were frankly motivated by hatred of the British and a burning desire to be rid of them. Outstanding amongst them was Rash Bihari Lall, who escaped to Tokyo in 1915 after an unsuccessful assassination attempt on Lord Hardinge. Through sheer doggedness he won the confidence of powerful Japanese, married and settled in Tokyo. This was later to gain him the reputation of a Japanese puppet, but in the meantime he formed what he called the Indian Independence League.

The Japanese clearly recognized the potential of this rather motley movement, which was to develop when war came. Under an intelligence officer, Major Fujiwara, was formed in 1941 the Fujiwara Kikan (agency), of rebel Indians.

Unknowingly the British helped, by failing miserably in Malaya in 1941, abandoning civilians, other than their own, and in some cases even them. Officers and men surrendered, including large numbers of Indians. After the fall of Singapore and the handing over by Colonel Hunt of many Indian troops to the Japanese, the Indian National Army was born – the INA, brainchild of Captain Mohan Singh and Major Fujiwara. It seized the opportunity of British humiliation to press the cause of a Free India.

The prime mover – whose name has also gone into legend – was Subhas Chandra Bose. Born into a large, prosperous Bengali family, Bose went to Cambridge, then joined and later resigned from the prestigious Indian Civil Service. After that his direction never wavered; he threw himself headlong into the Independence Movement in 1940. Almost always at loggerheads with Gandhi, he felt betrayed by Nehru, and decided to form a splinter group in the Congress – Forward Bloc.

Like others he was frequently imprisoned and released and then, in 1942, made a daring escape by road, train, bus and air from Calcutta to Berlin. He was the one Indian militant who took his fight all over the world. In Berlin he wooed Hitler, unsuccessfully. He made a dramatic journey by submarine to Tokyo, where he assumed the title of Netaji or leader. He travelled intensively, courting and cajoling, and succeeded in making the INA a formidable propaganda machine. His activities included raising a symbolic women's 'Rani of Jhansi' regiment, and he won many pledges from the Japanese, although it is doubtful whether these were intended to be kept. When he died, mysteriously – supposedly in a plane crash in 1945 – he became a legend, and remains a mystery.

For obvious reasons the British were at pains not to publicize the existence of this INA movement. Gandhi and the Congress were embarrassment enough in the middle of a war. To have proclaimed the existence of a militant expatriate force of their own renegade soldiers operating under enemy authority would have been an insufferable complication. Even when the whole thing was over the INA interlude was never emphasized. Bose was a very important Indian nationalist leader but little is made of him even now. He was an early and patriotic Congressman, far to the left of Gandhi, a straightforward classical revolutionary, and became President of Congress in 1939. But his ingrown militancy was never reconciled to what he called the Gandhi negativism and compromise.

The end of the war came sooner than expected. An INA thrust on Imphal, in Assam, was expensive in terms of lives and in any case abortive. Yet morale remained high. With hindsight it might have been a combination of genuine patriotism, propaganda and burnt bridges. Before the euphoria had died there suddenly came the Bomb, and Japan surrendered. Bose disappeared on 17 August 1945.

For the luckless rebels of the Indian National Army things were not so easily

4 AUGUST 1947

11

DAYS LEFT TO PREPARE FOR TRANSFER OF POWER

resolved. Their patrons the Japanese had let them down by surrendering. Their guiding light Subhas Bose had disappeared. There was nowhere to go but home. And no one could tell what would happen there.

British India was now almost out of hand. The upsurge of popular feeling was now irresistible. Even the Forces were showing signs of indiscipline reminiscent of the nineteenth century. No sooner had the war ended than the Indian Navy staged a mutiny in the harbour of Bombay, and actually trained its guns on the famous Taj Mahal Hotel on the seafront. The revolt was half-hearted and very swiftly fell to bits, but it was an ominous sign. Clement Attlee sent out the final Cripps mission. Independence – *Swaraj* – was now inevitable. The INA mutineers were an embarrassing complication, but something had to be done about them.

Just as the Nuremberg Trials were the post-war drama of Europe, so were the INA trials in India, and they were to prove the nails in the coffin of British rule. The sun which never set was swiftly clouding over. The likelihood of non-violent struggle being overtaken by national rebellion was not lost on the politicians in Britain. India was too remote to govern, and was now too poor and over-populated to be of any use to war-exhausted Britain.

Many generals, including Wavell, wanted to make an example of the INA men. The Commander-in-Chief, Auchinleck, was more compassionate, and probably wiser. The sheer logistics of trying thousands of men were by now beyond the capability of the British in India. However, a face-saving token trial was decided upon in Delhi's historic Red Fort – always the symbol of India's nationhood. Newspapers carried hardly any other stories; every literate man, woman or child read every word. Most important of all, the national leaders threw their full support behind their compatriots in the dock. They had used different methods, but towards the same goal. Gandhi did not attend the trial, but was never far

The count-down Below the sign telling them that Independence creeps on apace, the Viceroy Lord Mountbatten and his staff consult on the niceties of how to get out gracefully.

93

Chowpatty, on the seafront of Bombay, alternated as a pleasure-beach and a great arena for demonstrations. In March 1947 a vast crowd stoned the police who were breaking up an illegal meeting. Seventeen people were arrested.

away. Nehru and the most formidable brains made up the defence team. The defence hinged on the right of a subject people to wage war for their liberation. The defendants of the first trial were, symbolically, a Muslim, a Sikh and a Hindu. There were riots and demonstrations. All were found guilty. All were released after the trial. Other trials followed with almost always the same humiliating compromise; Indian military disaster became political victory. There was now nothing left but for the British to go, if possible, with dignity.

And so it came about. The Raj had come in with the gun, and it left with grace. Or so we thought.

All this largely left out of account the Princely States, which still occupied more than a third of all India. These were the great anachronism – the independent feudal relics of the past, the little monarchies which everyone accepted as being anachronisms but which somehow obstinately endured.

A wealth of romantic folklore had accreted around these strange mini-monarchs and their eccentric lifestyle. They were the rulers of their lands, sometimes minute and sometimes vast. There were legends that they wore priceless jewellery in bed and, it was said, conducted their daily business of despotism from the backs of richly-caparisoned elephants in more-than-oriental splendour. Another school of thought, mainly their own or that of their public-relations advisers, maintained that the Indian Princes were far-sighted and benevolent rulers and that their abolition would be a terrible mistake. However that might have been (and being an Indian affair it was naturally a bit of both) the Princes hung on to their privileges, stubbornly fighting on two fronts, against mythology on the one hand and democracy on the other.

A great deal of nonsense has been talked about the princely houses of India, their image everything from the romantic to the ridiculous. Sometimes their wealth and power were absurdly exaggerated; quite often they were in fact too fantastic to be exaggerated. The truth was that their privileges varied greatly. As late as 1971 there were still half a dozen rulers drawing Privy Purses of more than a million rupees, or £55,000; eighteen pulling down up to half a million. The Maharajah of Mysore, who was an austere and scholarly man with a good administrative record, had a Purse of some £140,000 a year, tax free. The Maharajahs of Jaipur, Baroda, Patiala and Travancore each got up to £90,000. This went on in a declining but scrupulously calculated scale until it reached rock bottom with a remote and half-forgotten Raja of Kotadia, whose Privy Purse of 192 rupees worked out at about ten pounds a year. This luckless man, who cycled to work every day as a municipal clerk in Gujerat, was from time to time invited to occasions befitting his meagre standing, but complained that no one ever sent him the fare.

The famous Nizam of Hyderabad, heir to a hugely celebrated miser who was allegedly among the four richest men on earth, had been chopped down to less than half of his predecessor's Purse, but was nevertheless worth more than £100,000 a year in public tax-free money. The average Indian income at the time (1971) was reckoned at £48 a year.

Then there were the famous Privileges. The Privy Purse, whatever it might be, paid no Income Tax. There was the title of His Highness, which was not only a matter of esteem but carried with it such amenities as free medical care for themselves, their families and their animals, free water and electricity, exemption from car taxes and gun-licences, the provision of armed guards for their Palaces; they could still demand their gun-salutes to reinforce their ego. When they passed on to their next *avatar* they could confidently expect full military honours at their funeral.

It took a long time, but eventually in Mrs Gandhi's time it became apparent that all this was preposterous in a nation professing the doctrine of the Mahatma and Nehru, and their regimes were ended. Democratic India was relieved. And as for the Rulers, most of them had long ago sent their capital abroad.

The relationship between the Indians and the British was a thing of great subtlety and even a kind of decorum; nobody else in the world could quite understand it, let alone define it. It was without rules or even recognized conventions. It was not colonialism, although it had colonial aspects, especially in administration. It was not comradeship, although here and there that feeling developed strongly. It was certainly not equality, because the very intrinsic nature of Hinduism precluded that; the anomalies of the caste-system had centuries ago divided and stratified Indian society itself into a variety of nations within a nation.

The British in India inhabited a country of – at the time between the wars – some three or four hundred million people, the huge majority of them illiterate and virtually penniless. They were a background scene – a pervasive and inescapable background, to be sure, but with few exceptions not to be taken on personal terms. It was acceptable to have a relationship with a personal servant, a bearer or a butler, out of the half-dozen domestics that usually formed a middle-class European family's household, but it was at the best paternal and remote.

There was of course the other India, that of the literate, the English-speaking merchant and business community, sometimes of great means, who in general terms were socially acceptable or even, if they happened to be both rich and Rajah-class (since almost a quarter of India was still technically under Princely rule), even desirable. Yet even to the end East was East and West was West, and the twain encountered each other on specified and recognized terms.

For the majority of middle-class Indian-English it was a good life. It may not

have been wholly the *dolce vita* it was cracked up to be, but it was certainly a lot nearer to it than most of them would ever have known in their own land, and by the time of the 'Raj Quartet' virtually everything had been taken for granted.

The principal factor was the – then – abundance of spacious accommodation and the availability of cheap and accessible domestic services. For example, a fairly modest European family, of managerial status that at home in Esher would have been glad of a regular daily help, would as a matter of course dispose of a head bearer, who supervised and often personally employed the staff; an *ayah*, or nurse; a *dhobi*, or laundryman; a *bhisti*, or sweeper-cum-water-carrier; a *mahli*, or gardener. This would have been considered fairly minimal; the somewhat more exalted would multiply their cast of characters by two or three times, until when you reached the top Indian Civil Service (let alone Viceregal) establishments the list could go into scores, if not hundreds.

This proliferation of domestic endeavour derived from (a) the poverty of the people, making any kind of income – however small – a thing to be cherished, and (b) the fact that the lower the social rating of the job the closer its rules. In India the educated could do many things, run many businesses, diversify and prosper, but the baser workers were and are specialists of the most precise and narrow kind; the more menial task the more exclusive its nature. A room-bearer can carry a flask of water but not a cup of tea; a floor-sweeper can brush the cigarette-ash to float up and subside, but he may not clean the toilet. The rules are inviolable, custom and caste and route and rote; to each his appointed small hierarchical place in the system, as it was in the beginning and evermore shall be. Thus every domestic operation however elementary will be divided and subdivided into strata of activities, each one so trifling that it could not in reason demand a living wage, requiring at the bottom but the clear performance of servility, to be seen in demonstrable lowliness on the floor or in the shadows to remind its betters that an established society always admits of one step lower.

This is *dharma*, the duty that is at the core of Hinduism – the distillation of virtue and hope for a better life after death in the eternal cycle of re-birth, the acceptance of any condition, since the more abject that condition the greater chance of its improvement.

The fatalism of the Indian poor is not apathy but dissociation, just as the indifference of the well-to-do is not callous or cynical, but an equal acceptance of the *dharma* that feeds some and starves others.

One would have thought that this was not a concept easily accepted by the English under-manager's wife from Bromley or Basingstoke. Yet by the final days of the Raj every minor Memsahib was saying: 'Let the *dhobi* look after that', or 'Leave it for the *bhisti*'. Here was a subtle paradox: the European had usurped the land, but India was infiltrating the tongue. It was done for no reason of intelligibility or convenience; it was a lingua franca to show that you were not a tourist or a visitor, but a pukka Mem, with a stake in the land.

The imprint of language became indelible. It is impossible to overhear a conversation between two literate Indians without noticing every few seconds the intrusion of an English word, for which there is no local translation, accepted and absorbed into every Indian tongue. The reverse process was subtler, and indeed less recognized. The soldiers' word for their own homeland, indeed, derived strictly from the Hindi – 'Blighty', from *bilayati*, or foreign. I am indebted to Geoffrey Moorhouse for his partial catalogue of English words stemming exactly from the Indian: bangle, bungalow, calico, chintz, chit, chutney, cushy, dinghy, dungaree, gymkhana, jodhpurs, kedgeree, khaki, lascar, loot, pyjama, sandal, shawl, swastika, tonga, verandah, yoga . . .

The number and variety of the Indian languages and scripts brought about the British invention of a bastard speech called 'Hindustani', derived from Urdu and Hindi. There was a quite celebrated and widely-used phrasebook, itself most revealing of the inter-racial relationships. It was 'Specially Composed For Visiting Persons And Allied Officers' by one H. Achmed Ismail, and it suffered from the

Oh, Calcutta The luckless Bengal city suffers again. A great mobilization of British troops could not prevent deadly riots on the Muslim festival of Id ul'Futr. Bodies litter the main street of Chitpore Road, including many women and children. On that August day in 1946 it is thought that 3,000 died.

The morning after The appalling Calcutta riots had subsided. Lord Wavell, the Viceroy (pointing), hears from a British officer of the bloodshed of the past few days among the rubbled streets. Luckily the Rolls awaits.

incurable complaint of all phrasebooks designed for communication between master-race and lesser breeds; it was unable to think otherwise than in brusque and peremptory commands: 'Come here. Go away. Cook more quickly and more better the tiffin. Wash more. Wake up. Stand still. Bring me instantly tea/coffee/whisky-soda/ammunition/daughters/vinegar. Do not lie. Go. Stay.' There was no tense but the imperative, no mood but the irascible. There was a fearsome chapter on The Engagement of Body-Servants: 'Look Sharp. Shut the Door. What is your Pay? I Shall Pay You Far Less. Put on the Fan. Put off the Fan. You feign Sickness. Make clean yourself. You are underdone. You are too old/too young. I shall engage another Bearer.'

Even in the 'Sickness' section Mr Achmed Ismail maintained a choleric impatience: 'The bowel is distracted. The tongue is hairy. I demand my teeth to be drawn.'

The personality of the disillusioned Mr Ismail permeated the book, with a wry satisfaction putting into the masters' hands every assistance for their natural bad manners.

This was not a parody, but a symptom.

Over the years the English language developed an obvious advantage to the Indians: it began to allow them to talk to each other. In a country with fourteen different and recognized local languages – many written in mutually incomprehensible scripts – the alien imposition became the only common tongue. It is not impossible – though some Indian zealots will disagree – that by far the most influential factor of change imposed upon India, the great influence on unification and indeed nationalism – was the English language. To the comparatively few Indians who came to know and read it in the early days it opened an enormous range of doors – to literature, political institutions, rational science.

It did in fact wholly transform a custom-bound and narrow hierarchical society – and indeed totally create the new ideas of democracy, individualism, and the rule of law. None of these concepts was of Indian origin – indeed they often ran counter to most things Indians held to be natural law.

Far more Indians know and speak English now than ever did under British rule. It is not quite the same English, since it derived from a generation of colonial Englishmen perhaps sixty years ago, and is often today a parody of Edwardianism, especially in officialese. So even with Independence India never shook off the British. It was partly imitation, and partly inertia.

There were to be sure the other British, officials and missionaries and Army officers who took their functions seriously and learned the language, but they were rarely found among the bridge-playing ladies, the Mems.

Thus two communities lived together, in parallel, mutually dependent but rarely coalescing. Whatever Gandhi said, they could not have got on without one another – or not during the Jewel days. This was not politics; it was social expediency. There were the Natives here, and the Rulers there. And between them existed a third society, of huge importance but disregarded for generations. They were The Others.

Two hundred years before the last days of the Raj, when India was simply a commercial branch of a British business, the East India Company had become aware that its exiled servants were human beings, and had accommodated them by shipping out European women in considerable numbers. This became eventually too expensive even for John Company, who not only condoned its men taking Indian wives and mistresses, but actively encouraged it. By the end of the eighteenth century the 'offspring of those unions', as they were delicately known, far outnumbered the pure-blood British.

They were defined in euphemisms – the Indo-British, Eurasians, East Indians, or sometimes even the Country-Born. Only in the census of 1911 were they officially defined as they thereafter remained: Anglo-Indians. As was inevitable, they had a rough time from both sides. The Europeans despised them – needing

OPPOSITE
Freedom at midday Calcutta is the biggest and busiest city in India, and Harrison Road is the biggest and busiest street in Calcutta. Now the tricolour flag is out for Independence Day, and so is everyone else.

Relationship between ruler and ruled was subtle and adaptable. Only in the hunting jungle was it unequivocal (A); the tiger and its decoy at least knew who was master. At the Viceroy's garden party in Belvedere Palace in Calcutta the encounter between Lord Linlithgow and the Maharaja of Patiala (B) was more delicate; this was still in the 1930s. Back in New Delhi in the war, part of Viceregal Lodge became a Leave Camp for soldiers (C). Officers, on the other hand, played polo; this was the famous ground at Ootacamund ('Ooty'), the southern hill-station (D).

At the races in Bombay in 1932 two Indian ladies of high degree (E) keep counsel together, but alone.

A

B

E F   C   D

H

Caste Hindus always refused
to work as air-hostesses; it was a
job reserved almost exclusively
for the Anglo-Indians, or mixed
blood (F).

A nice piece of symbolism:
the watchman of Viceregal
Lodge (G) in Simla with his
enormous collection of keys.

The ships' passage to India
regularly brought out their
cargoes of young memsahibs-
to-be (H) seeking what they
might find in the way of mates.
They were known as the
Fishing Fleet.

as they did someone to despise, since they could hardly despise the Indians on whose land they lived – and by their own people they were excommunicated. An Indian girl accepting a relationship with a European was renounced by her family and put 'out of caste'.

The British were – wisely – much more tolerant. Indeed many of these Anglo-Indians reached the top levels in the administration, and their names were famous even after Independence. For example Lord Roberts, British Supreme Commander in the Boer War, was the grandson of a Rajput princess. There were many such examples.

By the last years of the eighteenth century, however, the Company became alarmed at the growth of their Anglo-Indians, and barred mixed blood from recruitment to any other than menial jobs – except, of course, for those (and there were many) who had distinguished and even enriched themselves in the Government service. The Anglo-Indians in general found themselves in the most invidious of positions, ignored by the Anglos and despised by the Indians. They submitted to the epithets of *chi-chi*, from their accents, or *Kucha Bucha*, which meant 'half-baked bread'.

It came to pass, then, with encouragement from the British, that most Anglo-Indians came to man the Posts and Telegraphs departments, the Customs and Excise, and, almost totally, the swiftly expanding Railways. The Indian Railways became, and remained until the end of the Raj and even after that almost a monopoly employment of the Anglo-Indians. Everyone in the Paul Scott era knew that the ubiquitous Railway Institutes over the country were the central point everywhere of the Anglo-Indian community – and therefore of course, to be avoided by all but the most adventurous of sahib-society.

The huge error this community made long ago was to ignore or avoid the growth of the Indian Nationalist movement. There was an intrinsic snobbism among the Anglo-Indians that made them intuitively accept the white side – in politics as in dress and language and attitude. It has been said by historians of the time that if the Anglo-Indian leaders had cast their lot with the Indian Congress they could have been of great importance and influence. As it was, they fiddled about until almost the end, when Indian Independence was imminent, when they urgently and even desperately tried to unify into a coherent community, but it was too late, and they were sensitive enough to know it was too late.

As Independence became a certainty, thousands of them fled – some 25,000 to Australia and Canada, to start again in an environment just as uneasy and a climate far more hostile.

They need not have feared. The new Indian Constitution guaranteed them to some extent by recognizing their community as one of six official minority groups for which special provisions were codified in law – but only in as much as that of the lower castes, also protected by constitutional words. The Anglo-Indians were the truest victims of imperialism in that they never quite knew which side had let them down.

Another paradox about this great nation with a fierce pride in a varied past is that the major contribution to Indian records and history came from the strangers, the invaders, the uninvited conquerors. In the very first half-century of the British Raj it was oriental scholars like James Prinsep and Sir William Jones who saved the ancient history of India from oblivion. It can fairly be said that it was their British research and scholarship that stimulated, or even created, a sense of dignity and pride in educated Indians (by which one is obliged to mean English-educated Indians) and indeed created the nationalist movement that ultimately drove them out. It seems almost preposterously jingoist to say it now, but had it not been the British that colonized India, and indeed oppressed it, there would never have been a proud and free India today. Let that be our final smug remark.

It has been said that the major institution introduced to India by the British – after

Goodbye, home August 1947. Partition is accomplished; Lahore is no longer India. It is Muslim country now, and no place for Hindus and Sikhs. They crowd the wired-off platform and queue for the refugee train—the first of Pakistan's DPs. But by no means the last.

the Army, electric light, and the jute industry – was the Club. It was, perhaps, unique in the world. The Club was an empire within an Empire. Most of them came into being well after the Mutiny, in response to the obviously-growing impulse of Indian nationalism. They were enclaves of Englishness, both physically and psychologically. Here could be observed the Anglo-Saxon caste system at its best.

Hindu society was said to be hierarchical and rigidly divided, and it was, but the Sahibs ran it close. At the top were the Civil Servants and the Officers' Mess; at the bottom were the Other Ranks and NCOs of the Army, than which it was difficult to get lower. Between them, and harder to define, were the 'box-wallahs'. They were the white men who had settled in India to make money: they were in Commerce. Or, marginally worse, in Business.

These distinctions were of great moment to the committees of the Clubs, whose primary concern was exclusion rather than admission. Exclusion was determined by social status, politics, manners, and above all Race. Even the Clubs themselves had gradations. A junior box-wallah arriving in Calcutta (says Geoffrey Moorhouse, a great authority on Raj Clubdom) could join the Saturday Club with comparative ease, or even, in time, the Tollygunge Club, after hanging on the waiting-list for several years. He would have to have done very well for a very long time to achieve the Bengal Club 'where the atmosphere was more rarefied than anywhere else in the city'.

The Clubs inevitably became, to resentful Indians, the truly unacceptable face of Raj-dom. Shortly before Independence they would assemble outside the Delhi Gymkhana Club to jeer at the European members arriving formally in their dinner-jackets. 'Not long now!' they cried, and indeed it was not long. Independence came, and the Indians asserted their inalienable right to enter the Club, as a gesture of symbolic triumph.

They all wore dinner-jackets.

The other great institution contributed by the British to India – in this case benevolent rather than exclusive – was the phenomenon of the Hill Station. There were scores of them and, like everything imposed by the British for their own convenience, all more or less exactly the same. The Hill Stations were another demonstration of how the Raj could adapt anything, including the climate, to its own ends.

For more than a century the arrival of the Summer, or more properly the Hot Weather, was the signal for the European migration. Almost everything – the apparatus of Government, major commerce, social life – packed up and headed for the hills, to escape the intolerable heat of the cities of the plains. It was not an erratic holiday manoeuvre; it was a fact of administration. From May onwards India was governed not from Delhi but from Simla.

It was a remarkably sensible idea. Simla was several thousand feet up in the Himalayan foothills. The British had stumbled on it during the Gurkha wars, and never let it go. Lord Dufferin put up an extremely pretentious Viceregal Lodge – as the guide-book says: 'finely furnished by Maples of Tottenham Court Road'. For the Hot Weather period the Indian Empire was governed from here.

And it was to Simla that Sir Stafford Cripps' Cabinet Mission in 1946 summoned the hierarchy of Congress and Indian political leaders to consult over the tormenting detail of Independence, alternating between the magnificence of Viceregal Lodge and the out-of-town cottage Congress had rented for Gandhi.

Not all Hill Stations achieved the grandeur of Simla. That was not their intention. They were principally cool places to which exhausted Englishmen could retreat and persuade themselves that they were back in Horsham, with India long ago and far away. By far the most celebrated of the southern ones was Ootacamund, seven thousand feet up in the Nilgiris – the famous 'Ooty' of the Raj legend – which the British had chosen for its local resemblance to the English Home Counties. They emphasized the likeness by renaming everything nostalgically. The town centre was called Charing Cross. The little villas everywhere bore the sentimental names of Runnymede, Torquay, even Harrow-on-the-Hill. And what is more, they still do.

Only by this kind of sad charade could the English, and especially the English ladies, reconcile themselves to having lost the bridge-parties of Tunbridge Wells. For of course they had done nothing of the kind; they had merely transferred them. Edwardian England lingered on in India long after the twentieth century and, above all, the War, had extinguished it at home. It did no special harm to India. It just created a special species of Brits, whom no one will ever see again.

The bowing-out of the British Raj from the continent of India was a phenomenon unprecedented in imperial history. In the following years we were to see other European nations abandon their colonies reluctantly, bloodily, and with huge bitterness. It took the Dutch in the East Indies two more years of angry battle to become convinced that Indonesia no longer wanted them. As late as 1960 the Belgians were still fighting furiously to hang on to the Congo. The French had to be defeated in an especially horrible war finally to leave Algeria in 1962. Even more bitterly, the Portuguese clung to Angola until the guerrilla force finally expelled them in 1975.

After two centuries of a foreign domination the Indian people found themselves free to do what they wished and go where they wanted – and on achieving Independence at once opted for Dominion status under the Crown, precisely as that of Canada, Australia and New Zealand. Even when they decided formally to become a Republic in 1950 they asked to remain within the British Commonwealth. Even more, India asked the last Viceroy to stay on in New Delhi as Governor-General of the Dominion, which Lord Mountbatten did for almost a year. Other senior British administrators, including the Governors of Bombay and Madras, also remained for some time at the request of the Nehru Government. This eagerness to cling on to political connections was not the attitude of a resentful people gladly liberated from an oppressive overlord.

Indeed when India became a Republic its first President, Rajendra Prasad, said it was 'the consummation and fulfilment of the historic tradition and democratic ideals of British rule'. The first Indian Constitution adopted the British parliamentary form of government, if only because the Indians tried no other. At the time it seemed sage and reasonable although every serious Indian politician now agrees that the methodology needs revision and change.

In fact the British left India with a multitude of problems. Most of them had existed throughout the Raj and long before. Caste endured, with its attendant injustices and cruelties, even though the 1950 Constitution expressly refused to recognize caste distinctions and forbade the practice of Untouchability. Money-lenders flourished and proliferated; corruption remained as general as ever in places low and high. The distribution of wealth remained fantastically unequal, with the few enjoying a grotesque level of luxury and the vast majority existing in dreadful poverty. The police remained deeply suspect of corruption. The memory of Mahatma Gandhi faded by the year.

It is perfectly true that the early Imperialists were motivated by greed, and managed the Indian economy strictly for their own benefit and not India's. Nevertheless in the final years of their dominion the British guided the Indian economy to the point where, by the start of the Second World War, it had achieved a favourable balance of trade with the UK. Indian industry was to some degree protected from the more powerful British competition.

The enduring illustration of this was the great Parsi family Tata, the head of which formed the Indian steel industry back in 1907. His descendants so vigorously expanded it that by the year of Independence Tata's was worth £54 million and employed 120,000 people. It started India off into heavy industry, where it still significantly remains.

What else, in fact, did the British Raj bequeath to India?

Materially, a great deal, enduring and visible today, in public works all over the land: great systems of railways, roads, irrigation, plantation. It was the institution of communications that made possible a united nation – or as united as such a varied and mixed-up society could ever be. In the early nineteenth century most public works were directed at the reduction of famine, which had always been the curse of a heavily-populated country where the rainfall could vary from more than 450 inches a year in the Assamese highlands to a desperate three inches in Sind, and which nowhere could be relied on because of the erratic monsoon.

Even the Moguls had realized that irrigation must be the answer to this, and had dug some rudimentary canals, which had decayed swiftly as the Mogul authority faded. In the 1820s the British began to restore them, and indeed multiply them. Lengths of the Ganges were canalled over some four hundred miles of desert. Similar watercourses were established in all the arid regions, especially in the dry and desolate Punjab. The process continued during all the period of the British occupation, and by the time of Independence in 1947 a fifth of all cultivable land in India was artificially irrigated.

Previous imperialisms had left their mark in isolated objects – the immortal Taj Mahal was the memorial one man created for his wife; it was beautiful and did nothing whatever for India in its time. It was left to an only half-remembered Governor-General, Lord Dalhousie, who came into the country in 1848, to transform the nation in practical ways that endure today.

The long good-bye Indian Independence—one day old. Lord Mountbatten, now Governor-General of the new Dominion of India, tours Delhi with Lady Mountbatten to say goodbye. Whatever relations had been for the past years, they were ecstatic now; the British were the most popular people in the world. The crowds broke the police cordon to swarm round the once-Viceregal coach to applaud and shake hands. Then the Mountbattens cruised on for a Council meeting.

In his six years of office Dalhousie created modern India. He initiated the vast system of telegraph wires, some four thousand miles of them, which as much as anything made the scattered mass of the subcontinent aware that it was a nation. And, of course, he helped create an arterial system that lingers today and without which there could have been no Indian nation – the railways.

Governor-General Dalhousie was an enthusiast, even a fanatic, of railways, which were a comparative novelty even in Europe in those days. But Dalhousie had been President of the Board of Trade before arriving in India and been much involved in railway development at home, and he brought his obsession to India.

The difficulties were enormous. Railways in Britain were a pushover compared to establishing them in a place the size and complication of India – enormous distances, wild climatic extremes, a land of vast mountains and daunting floods, not to speak of the capital investments required. The then East India Company grudgingly conceded him two experimental lines. Almost at once the Company disappeared. In 1869 the Government took over all responsibility for running the railways, or rather for delegating private companies to run them; in 1853 the Great India Peninsular Railway had sent off its historic first train of fourteen coaches from Bombay for its twenty-one-mile trip to Thana. It was the beginning of what was probably the most important social development the nation had ever seen.

The romance of the Indian Railways has been the subject of books and films for years, and rightly so. As with everything Indian, matters relatively simple elsewhere turned into extravagant complication. For the short run from Bombay to Surat eighteen river bridges had to be built, and foundations driven sometimes to 140 feet. The line through the Western Ghats needed twenty-two bridges and twenty-five tunnels to overcome a gradient of one in thirty-seven. It is said that forty thousand men were needed to drive the line through the Ghats, a third of whom never lived to see its end.

By Independence there were forty thousand miles of Indian railway track, varying in gauges as much as in ownership – the Great Eastern, the Bombay, Baroda and Central India (the famous BB & CI, whose initials still linger fadingly on some of the old coaches), the Madras, the Punjab, the Delhi, the Sind, the East Bengal, not to speak of the smaller personal railways built for the wealthier rulers of Indian States, occasionally with a personal throne in the main carriage.

These engineering works were the visible and tangible legacies of the Raj. Incidental to them, less material but hopefully equally enduring, was the huge concept still emerging – democracy.

The institution of an elected Parliamentary Government was the last of the legacies. It was, as every thinking Indian agrees, an unconscionable time in coming. It was, obstinately but perhaps understandably, resisted by the Raj almost until the end. The Indians were both ambitious and imitative; they argued that if the parliamentary system worked for the masters it could work for them, and by slow stages they achieved it, as nowhere else in the former colonial world ever did.

There was to be sure a tremendous hiccup in 1975, when the Prime Minister Indira Gandhi, daughter of the great Jawaharlal Nehru, feeling herself threatened by an excess of opposition, introduced laws of repression, censorship and political imprisonment that many Indians held to be worse than anything the British had done.

Yet to everyone's great surprise Indira Gandhi submitted her Government to a general election, which she resoundingly lost. And three years later was re-elected by a population wholly disillusioned by her opposition. As a contemporary historian wrote: 'If Independence had been India's proudest moment, that submission thirty years later should have run it a close second, for it was the assurance that even in the bleakest circumstances India would abide by its independent ideals.'

So it can be said, and repeatedly has been said, that what the British Raj left most importantly to India was the rule of law and the Parliamentary vision. The

Constitution India decreed for itself in 1950 left the British legal system almost unaltered and perfectly reproduced the inherited administrative machine – with all its efficiencies and all its faults.

Still, an administrative machine it was, and in pretty good working order. For years the British had been striving to liberalize the composition of the white-oriented ICS – the prestigious Indian Civil Service – by recruiting more and more Indians into the elite; but as the ICS strength rarely at any time counted more than a thousand this was not easy. Nevertheless, when Independence came the British-Indian ratio of the ICS was about fifty-fifty, and the vaster provincial service below it was almost entirely Indian. The last British intake into the ICS was in 1939.

India was not left, as so many ex-dependencies were to be left all over the world, groping its way through unfamiliar complications of government.

Nor was the new nation short of professional men, with some 90,000 registered doctors and at least 100,000 university teachers. There was an experienced and accomplished engineering industry, capable of manufacturing cars, locomotives, aeroplanes – and atom bombs. All this, and the solid infrastructure of communication: the language, irrigation, roads, and railways, constituted the not inconsiderable legacy of the Raj.

Perhaps the greatest and most imponderable element of the British inheritance – as we tend rather smugly to repeat – was the simple rule of law, plus of course the Parliamentary concept. The Constitution of 1950 derived greatly from the 1935 Government of India Act, with the addendum of a Bill of Rights that owed much to that of the United States. But almost the entire British legal system was adopted virtually unaltered. With an electorate (at the beginning) of just under 200 million people, and a viable and instructed Civil Service, India's Independence was in business in a way no other ex-colonial emergent nation in the world would ever be.

Why, then, did it not at once succeed?

Who is to say it did not?

The Raj was, and is, an unconscionable time in dying. True, the statue of George V disappeared from the Kingsway of New Delhi, very quietly and without ceremony; and similar images were removed all over the land. Yet there is still a remote and dismal field on the edge of Old Delhi where a dozen or so examples of such memorabilia are packed ingloriously side by side, forgotten names fading into ever more anonymity; India does not want them but is too polite to smash them up. To many people interested in Anglo-Indian political relationships there is something very touchingly symbolic about this. There is scarcely a town in all India that has not some building, most probably a Council Chamber or a Post Office, that recalls its counterpart in Huddersfield or Barnsley.

The British introduced the game of cricket; it became – and remains – a national

addiction, attracting crowds of a size and enthusiasm to be seen nowhere else on earth. It could be said that India did an exchange deal with polo, but polo is an elitist game hardly to be compared.

It was inevitable that Britain should have brushed off on India far more than the reverse. Architecturally there are far more Macclesfields in India than there are Bhowanis in Britain, though there remains the Brighton Pavilion, the delightfully dotty extravaganza designed to delight the Prince Regent with its oriental absurdity. There was a cross-fertilization, but it was mainly one-way.

That was until the Indian restaurants arrived . . .

All this is of course the trimming on the cake, the fairly superficial decoration illustrating a relationship that went far deeper, as the personal jargon of a close family establishes its own intimacies. For this was a parting not only without rancour or bitterness but actually with a grudging sense of regret.

In years to come India's fossilized officialdom did not just imitate the Raj: it even exaggerated its worst aspects of bureaucracy to the point where, more than thirty years later, liberal Indians can look back nostalgically to the accommodating ways of Empire.

These literate and ambitious Indo-Anglians are now obliged to live in two worlds at once. 'Advancing India' became like a man trying to climb a steep cliff with one foot tethered to a hole in the ground: his foot, strangely enough, quite happy where it was; that was his terrible trouble.

Nobody can yet be sure, nor ever will be sure, whether the Raj, the Indian Empire, that strange betrothal of East and West, of brown and white, of guns and gurus, was in lasting terms a good thing. It brought advantage and suffering, success and despair, hate and love – in the measure, indeed, of every human marriage.

Paul Scott remembered

1. ROLAND GANT, editor and first publisher of the 'Raj Quartet'

This is the story of a rape, of the events that led up to it and followed it and the
place in which it happened. . . . There was no trial in the judicial sense . . . [it]
ended with the spectacle of two nations in violent opposition, not for the first
time nor as yet for the last because they were then still locked in an imperial
embrace of such long standing and subtlety it was no longer possible for them
to know whether they hated or loved one another, or what it was that held them
together and seemed to have confused the image of their separate destinies.

Paul Scott, *The Jewel in the Crown*

What kind of life did Paul Scott lead? What manner of man was he? How was the
man related to the events which he took as his raw material and to the characters
he created?

Paul Mark Scott was born in Palmer's Green, north London, on 25 March 1920,
the younger of the two sons (there were no daughters) of Thomas Scott, a commercial artist, and his wife, Frances Mark Scott, also a commercial artist. Paul was
educated at Winchmore Hill Collegiate School and later began training as an
accountant. In 1940 he joined the army, the Royal East Kent Regiment, known as
The Buffs and formerly the 3rd of Foot. One of his friends, James Leasor the
writer, told me:

I first met Paul Scott in late 1942 or early 1943 at No. 148 Training Brigade – a pre-
OCTU at Wrotham. I think we shared a Nissen hut which was very cold and we burned
wood in the stove in the middle but because of the fumes in the night we all had to
urinate on the stove to put it out.

We arrived on Friday. Next day we were called out at noon to form a single line. The
camp was in the grounds of a former stately home and everyone fell in on the drive.
Scott and I were side by side. A sergeant-major with a pace-stick came down, staring
closely into the face of every individual after the manner of his kind. He reached Scott
and me, put his pace-stick to one side and told those beyond the stick to fall out. The
rest of us were on 'India Draft'. We were given embarkation leave until the following
Sunday.

On the troopship a call went out for anyone with journalistic or writing experience.
Scott and I stood forward and were given the task of helping with the daily ship's paper.

At the Officers Training School at Belgaum [in India] we also produced, with two or three others, a weekly wall newspaper.

Paul Scott was much more serious-minded than many of us, but he had a lighter side to his character.

My impression of him then was of someone unusually grave, composed, almost introverted, but underneath was a much livelier character trying to escape and finally did so with *Staying On*. In Belgaum was a small hotel, Green's. This, he told me, was the basis for the hotel in *Staying On*.

When the time came to pass out I still could not make any sense of Morse code, which was apparently essential, although I never used it thereafter. Scott couldn't understand the intricacies of the internal combustion engine. Since we wore a piece of cardboard with our number on our bush jackets and the examiners did not know us by name, it was easy for us to change places for the Morse code and MT tests. As a result, we both passed.

Scott and I were both writing novels in our spare time. I finally sold mine to an obscure publisher, sending it back bit by bit in airmail envelopes. I don't know what happened to his. It was then called *Brilliant City* – an excellent title I wish I had thought of – perhaps he revamped it into his first published book?

After the war, when I was on the *Daily Express*, I wrote a novel which was advertised in the *Bookseller*. Paul, who I had not seen for years, rang me up and asked if I was the James Leasor he had known. Thereafter we used to meet regularly every month at Ley On's Chinese Restaurant in Soho – now gone, like so much else. . . .

The sad thing, to my mind, is that all his working life he struggled with immense dedication and effort and then achieved fame and fortune after his death.

Here is one writer speaking from the heart about another. Scott was demobilized in 1946 and became company secretary of the Falcon Press, whose founder and chairman, Captain Peter Baker, MC (later Conservative Member of Parliament for South Norfolk), had published Scott's poems in his wartime poetry broadsheets. Associated with the Falcon Press was the Grey Walls Press, and the offices of these two publishing companies were situated in a narrow alleyway in the West End of London running between King Street, St James's, and Pall Mall. It was here, at 6 Crown Passage, Pall Mall, that Paul Scott and I met for the first time, he as newly-appointed company secretary and I as publicity manager and general dogsbody who believed I was filling in time between discharge from a military hospital and a return to France or departure to Canada.

In those days when ex-soldiers were scrabbling around for jobs, each of us was wary of the other and wary also of Peter Baker, who was intelligent, amusing, somewhat deranged and highly untrustworthy beneath a plausible manner. When we saw that his irresponsibilities (partly the result of his POW experiences) were leading the firm to disaster we realized we had to get out. Paul joined a firm of literary agents and I went to William Heinemann the publishers. This was in 1950.

Paul Scott spent ten years as a literary agent, first with Pearn, Pollinger and Higham and then, after a division of the firm into two, of David Higham Associates. During that time he established a reputation as an intelligent and sensitive author's agent, able to advise his clients not only on where to place their work but also on the work itself. It was during this time that we had what we called the most incestuous literary relationship in London. Paul was agent for my novels, he was agent for my wife Nadia Legrand (also a novelist), and he placed novels by *his* wife, who wrote as Elizabeth Avery, with Michael Joseph, of which house I was editorial director at the time. Only one thing remained to round off this literary family circle. One day I must publish Paul Scott.

During those years when Paul was published by one publishing house while I worked in others we remained close friends. I remember how my wife and I dined with the Scotts in their hedge-hidden house in Hampstead at the time when their two daughters were infants. The Scotts later moved to a larger house in Hampstead Garden Suburb where, in addition to their growing-up daughters, there was a prodigious family of cats of all sizes and colours who roamed the woodland behind the house when they were not petitioning for fish at the kitchen door.

Penny and Paul Scott even took for a while a large and pompous old cat called Moumoune who looked like Marshal Pétain and had to be left behind by my wife's parents when they returned to France in 1947 after their wartime exile in England. Paul always maintained that although Moumoune had been born here he disdained to understand a word of English.

It was in a first-floor room of that house in Addison Way, with a view of the garden, the trees beyond, the occasional prowling fox for whom Paul put out bread and milk at night, and, of course, a cat or two, that Paul Scott wrote his novels. After leaving the literary agency in 1960 to devote his time to writing he established a routine to which he adhered strictly. For some years he reviewed regularly for *Country Life* and occasionally for *The Times* and the *Times Literary Supplement*. This reviewing work and in fact all work that was not actually to do with the novel in hand he applied himself to at weekends. He took enormous care over his reviewing, bringing to whatever he did a high standard of critical appraisal to which was added his insight as an artist into what the writer was saying or trying to say.

In 1962 I joined the publishing company Secker and Warburg, part of the Heinemann group, who shortly published his novels *The Bender* (1963) and *The Corrida at San Felíu* (1964). Meanwhile Paul Scott was sticking to India in his own very private way. It was India and the problems of Anglo-Indian relationships that absorbed most of his waking time and, from what he told me, much of his sleeping time as well.

In the year of the publication of *The Corrida at San Felíu* we talked much about tropical diseases and the effect on the bodies and minds of those, particularly Europeans, who contracted them. I had had some fascinating experiences in this field, having contracted amoebic dysentery in a German prisoner-of-war camp which was cured many years later by the draconian methods employed by a Catalan-Indo-Chinese physician in Paris. I had become very interested in the side-effects of the disease and worked for a while with the physician in recording case-histories. It seemed to me that Paul Scott displayed the signs and symptoms of amoebiasis and had become somewhat desperate about his almost permanent ill-health. I took him to Paris where he was treated and cured, and he, the physician and I had many conversations about the psychological aspects of the disease – many of which, we agreed, were manifest in the stop-and-start methods and eroded will of Scott's character Edward Thornhill in *The Corrida*.

As Scott had undoubtedly contracted amoebiasis in India during the war there was an unwanted link with the past, and in 1964 he plunged into post-Partition India, his first visit for nearly twenty years. It was, in his own words, a valuable 'recharging of the batteries' made possible in part by money provided by his publishers. He got in touch with friends made during the war, established new contacts and all in all obtained a prodigious impetus from his visit.

Shortly after his return I rejoined the parent company Heinemann, and Scott's first novel to appear under this imprint was the one originally announced as the first of a trilogy, a novel that owed much to those batteries recharged in India, *The Jewel in the Crown* (1966).

The second novel of what Paul Scott could now see would be a quartet rather than a trilogy was *The Day of the Scorpion* (1969), and the circular shape that was to become so distinctive a feature of the 'Raj Quartet' began to be evident in the repetition of incidents seen from different viewpoints. At the beginning of 1969 Paul Scott paid another visit to India. One of his areas of research was, he told me, 'to get some fuller picture of the INA [Indian National Army] trials in the Red Fort in 1945-6'. In a letter to me from Bombay just before he left for New Delhi in mid-January 1969 he wrote: 'Have not yet settled to much work, but my researches into the INA are beginning to make some ground – if only confirmatory. One has to tread carefully because it is still a tricky subject [being the history of those Indians who had fought beside the Japanese during the war]. The general (Indian) I spoke to last night seemed a bit un-nerved.' This 'tricky subject' was handled superbly by Scott in the last volume of the 'Raj Quartet', *A Division of the*

Spoils. But that came out in 1975 and in between came the third novel, *The Towers of Silence*, published in 1971, a year before Paul Scott paid his final visit to India.

That visit was mainly to confirm earlier research and impressions, for the pattern of the Quartet was quite clear in his mind. He knew where he was going to place his characters and he also knew what happened to them after the last page of his work had been written. Not only did the Smalleys, minor characters in the Quartet, return to the stage in *Staying On*, having stayed on until 1972 from the time of Partition, but when I asked Paul, 'What happened to a Muslim politician like Kasim after Partition?', he answered without hesitation: 'Oh, he was persuaded to take on the Ministry of Agriculture three and a half years later' – as though I had requested information about a real-life Indian politician. Paul went on to tell me that he knew what happened to all the characters he had created. He did not say this in any portentous way but as a matter of fact, just as one might talk about old So-and-So at a Regimental Reunion.

Paul Scott did not have a particular affinity with Indians any more than he had a particular affinity with the British. There was no pukka sahib side to his character and neither was he in love with the romantic idea of past Imperial splendour. What interested him most of all was trying to understand why the British presence in India, which should have been a successful partnership, ended in recrimination, departure, division and bloodshed. The interplay, emotional and political, between the nations fascinated him as did the relationship between individuals as, for example, the love between the English-educated Indian Hari Kumar and the atypical memsahib Daphne Manners in *The Jewel in the Crown*. Their relationship was doomed to end in violence, injustice and death for Daphne when their child was born.

I realize that up to now I have shown Paul Scott as writer, creator and to some extent, perhaps, willing victim of his own creation. 'But what was he *like?*' is the question which I am always asked since his death by people all over the world, either in connection with academic theses or for background to critical articles or out of the commendable and natural curiosity of the devoted reader.

Well, what *was* he like? James Leasor has given an idea of Paul Scott in the early years of the war and on arrival in India. Mrs Paul Scott – Penny to everyone other than the reviewers of her Elizabeth Avery novels – said that she was engaged to marry somebody else when the twenty-one-year-old Paul Scott came along and insisted on their being married at once. They were, and he was then posted to the Far East for the next three and a half years while his wife, a nursing sister, worked and waited in England.

When we met in 1946 Paul Scott gave the impression of being quite tall and of slender build. This was deceptive, the illusion being aided by his angular face, smoothly-brushed dark hair and longish nose – an impression of a man tall and slim whereas in fact he was not much above average height and he was both broad-shouldered and muscular, this too hidden by his dark suit.

A cool, level gaze gave no hint of jumping to rapid conclusions; he had a quiet and level voice to match, and my overall first impression was that of a twenty-six-year-old man glad to get a job, as we all were in those post-war years of ex-servicemen tumbling around in their demob suits, trying to find some way of making a living. Little by little I got to know him better, in the pub across the passage over a pint or two, on a few excursions or lunches with authors or at dinner with our wives. Books we had read and authors we admired filled much of the conversation as did books we disliked and writers we detested: the war writers who had survived and those who had perished – and many of those who had perished survived strongly as writers and some of those who had survived the war perished as writers in peacetime. There was a lot of music too, listened to and talked about – Wagner, Mozart, Elgar, the Ink Spots, Fats Waller, Louis Armstrong, blues singers like Bessie Smith – and bits of old Hollywood dialogue were thrown back and forth, with arguments as to words and intonation, story-line and date. We collected bizarre names – the British Council provided a rich seam in these – and invented meetings between literary or public figures, improvising discussions in which each misunderstood what the other was really saying. We used to write obituaries of each other, getting details subtly wrong as so often happens in the obit. world. We agreed to put a stop to this because, as Paul said, 'One day one of us will snuff it and the other will be asked to write an obituary and, looking through a drawer, probably pissed at the time, find one and send it off. It will get printed and nothing, no amount of letter-writing and corrections will ever get it put right.'

Our wives had a lot to put up with in the course of these cabaret turns which we ourselves found so hilarious at the time that tears of laughter fell into the drinks that were always in hand in large measure.

Paul Scott was not only a witty but a very funny man – and the two do not always go together. He had a sharp and mocking sense of humour, a gift for mimicry in both tone of voice and choice of words. Finding something amusing in the newspapers – a pompous figure coming to grief or an academic uttering inanities – would send us to the telephone to invent the consequences, the 'questions in the House', ways of taking an idiocy mock-seriously and making mischief out of it. I suppose we wasted a lot of each other's time but it was time well wasted and took the gritty edge off our lives which, as we grew older, seemed to offer less and less to laugh about. Neither of us ever had much money and we were always having to grub around while children were growing up and mortgages were being paid. We complained to each other about the underpayment for demanding journalism and the general grinding down which applied to us as it did to thousands of others. We were both very lucky in having wives who while chiding us for alcoholic excesses and inexcusable eruptions of bad temper were themselves writers who showed more indulgence than they need have done.

In my preface to Paul Scott's short story 'After the Funeral' – which I shall mention later – I wrote the following paragraph:

There was a strong family element in our friendship in which we shared the pleasure in our wives' writing, in our respective children's ambitions and progress, the aims and problems of authorship, the shortcomings of critics and the vagaries of publishing. To most discussion Paul brought a kind of lugubrious gaiety that was composed of mocking cynicism, hilarity in the contemplation of human vanity, trendiness and pomposity and a loathing of the phoney. Different in many ways, we shared a number of faults such as unpredictable moodiness that makes one very difficult to live with and shared occasions of drinking to a Celtic pattern which once took us in the very early morning to Oxford in an ancient motor-car. The spires were dreaming yet and there was nothing to do but kick a college wall or two because we were not a quarter of a century younger and were very much down rather than up. A bunch of wilted bluebells gathered on the way back and proffered by a shaky hand did nothing to help our homecoming.

How did Paul Scott and I eventually work so successfully together as author and publisher? First of all because we understood each other very well in this near family relationship that developed over thirty years and our discussions were always honest and to the point. When there was something in one of his books which I had failed to understand, either because the meaning was so veiled in ambiguities or because I was thick and had missed the point, we would talk about it, act out the parts, speak the dialogue, invent what this or that reviewer would say about it, until we agreed that the best form and shape had been achieved.

Paul Scott kept well away from the London literary scene and its mutually congratulatory cliques. To some extent this refusal to go out and about and take part in the back-scratching stakes put a brake upon the recognition of Paul Scott as a major novelist. There were, it is true, percipient reviewers all along the way who saluted the exceptional quality of his work. Susan Hill in *The Times* referred to 'one of the most important literary landmarks of post-war fiction . . . a mighty literary experience', and David Holloway, literary editor of the *Daily Telegraph*, called Scott's novels 'a portrait of the real India'.

On one of his rare public appearances on the London literary scene Scott gave a talk entitled 'India: a post-Forsterian View' to the Royal Society of Literature of which he was elected a Fellow. This talk was later published in *Essays by Divers Hands* (Royal Society of Literature, 1970). He felt this exercise was worthwhile, but the ordinary cocktail party he considered to be a terrible bore and waste of time.

It was, he admitted, flattering to be invited as Visiting Lecturer to the University of Tulsa, Oklahoma, in 1976. His sales had never been enormous in the United States, but such a visit might help. He enjoyed enormously his first teaching visit to Tulsa, and the presence of this apparently diffident, quirky and immensely intelligent and amusing English lecturer was much appreciated. So much so that he was invited to return the following year.

Before returning to Tulsa Paul completed and saw published his last novel, *Staying On*. I found then, in 1977, and still find whenever I look at it, the dedication 'To my old colleague and friend Roland Gant whom I regard and thank' immeasurably moving. My wife and I gave a party in our house for the book's publication. Paul was already a sick man. He suspected it and we half-suspected it. Just before leaving for Tulsa he said to my wife: 'I am so tired, so tired. I don't know if I'll ever get there or, if I do, if I'll ever get back here again.'

It was while recovering from surgery for cancer in Tulsa that Paul Scott was awarded the Booker Prize for Fiction in November 1977. His elder daughter, Carol, who accepted the prize on his behalf, went to Oklahoma, and her affection, intelligence and cheerful personality did much, so Paul told me, to get him into a state where he was able to return to England for Christmas that year. His younger daughter Sally illustrated Paul's short story 'After the Funeral', published in a limited edition by the Whittington Press in 1979. (Paul did not live long enough to see the proofs of this book but Sally went on to make a name for herself as a designer and illustrator.) It was typical of Paul Scott to say, a few days before he died: 'I picked a good title in "After the Funeral", didn't I?' But as I wrote in the preface to that story: ' "I love life," Paul told me when he had only a few days left. His intelligence, intuition and intellectual wholeness still make him much more alive to me than are many of the living.'

Paul Scott died of cancer in the Middlesex Hospital, London, on 1 March 1978. We had talked a few days before on Granada's plans to film *Staying On* for television – and at the preview I felt how much he would have approved of it – and of the possibilities of the 'Raj Quartet' being brought to the screen. He seemed to have little doubt that this would eventually happen and said how much he would like to have had a hand in it. But of course he did, because without Paul Scott there would be neither book nor television series.

2. M. M. Kaye

World War II had been over for close on seven years, and what has come to be known as 'the Raj' had ended for almost five by the time that I first met Paul Scott. He was then a young man, barely in his thirties and already making his mark as a writer, while I was what an American was later to describe (accurately!) as 'a left-over from the Raj', who had written a few children's books and three 'Whodunits'.

It was the third of these – a murder story set in Kashmir – that was responsible for our meeting: though I cannot remember to this day why or how I came to pick on the particular literary agents for whom he was working. Someone must have mentioned them to me. Or perhaps I merely used a pin? – probably the latter. But the result was, for me, one of the greatest pieces of luck that has ever come my way.

The manuscript having been favourably received, I was asked to come to London to discuss it, and, on arrival, handed over to a young man who was introduced to me as Mr Scott. It seemed that he had been selected to look after my interests solely because he had served, toward the end of the war, in India, and my novel happened to be set in one of India's princely States. We sat down and talked about the possibilities of the book and what he suggested we do with it, and after about ten minutes of this the interview was over and I shook hands and left.

I cannot have taken more than half-a-dozen steps when I was struck by a sudden thought. I stopped and turned round, and asked if his first name was Paul. He said it was, so I enquired if by any wild chance he had written a book called *The Alien Sky*. He had indeed. So I said that, in that case, could I please shake his hand again, because I'd enjoyed it enormously. His reply to this was a blank 'Good God!', and when I asked what that was in aid of, he said that on a snap judgement he'd have thought I would have hated the book. My reply to this was: 'Oh dear, did I really come across as some sort of "Poona-Poona Memsahib"?' At which he shouted with laughter, and we were friends from that moment on.

It proved, for me, a most valuable and entertaining friendship. And one which gave me much to be thankful for, quite apart from the help and encouragement I received from him in the way of business. My husband being in the Army, I spent much of my time abroad in all sorts of entertaining bits of Britain's fast vanishing Empire, but Paul was an excellent correspondent and we kept in touch by letter. He would write to me from India, when he began to go out there on sponsored tours, and his letters were always interesting and frequently hilarious, for he had a marvellous sense of humour. And as everyone knows, his descriptions of people and places, and his eye for detail, were Grade A plus.

He never once tried to influence or alter the way in which I write – bar attempting to ration me to one exclamation mark per page. But he gave me endless tips on how to deal with the sticky patches and the quicksands that writers like myself frequently get bogged down in. His advice on how to get back onto dry land was invaluable, and had it not been for this, I suspect that I would still be struggling somewhere half-way through *The Far Pavilions*.

He told me once that his ambition had been to be a poet, and that he had become a writer by mistake. Which was something I could fully understand and sympathize with, since I too had become a writer by mistake, having meant to be an illustrator of children's books – a second Rackham or Edmund du Lac. He was also very musical, which, alas, I am not, and could have made a Mike Yarwood-fortune in the theatre or on TV by his ability to mimic anyone, and take them off to the life.

I have met many people who assume that because of his obsession with India, Paul must have spent many years in that country, and probably had more than a touch of Indian blood in his veins. But this was not so. His first sight of that country was when he arrived there with his unit, which had been posted to India to help in the jungle war against the Japanese. And he had fallen in love with it in exactly the same way as, very many years before, my father had fallen madly in love with China, where his regiment had been sent to clear up the mess left by the Boxer Rising. There is no explaining this sort of love-affair, any more than one can explain why certain men and women fall in love with each other. It happens, and that's all there is to it.

Paul saw little or nothing of the 'Raj', and his own choice for an overall title for the Quartet was, according to a joke in one of his letters, *Cash and Curry*. The India he saw was not the true 'Raj', for by that time the lines had become blurred by the war, and also by the fact that everyone knew that as soon as that war was over, the next thing on the agenda would have to be the end of the Raj and freedom for India. This was the epoch that Paul saw and wrote about: and if, in a hundred or three hundred years from now, anyone wants to know exactly how it was then, they will be able to find out by reading 'The Raj Quartet'. It is all there – for as long as libraries exist and men and women are interested in the past.

I think that what Paul liked about me was the fact that I had actually seen the real 'Raj': had lived in its hey-day, and belonged to a family who had served India for several successive generations – an 'India' family, one of whose members had written *A History of the Afghan War* (the first Afghan War) and a contemporary history of the Indian Mutiny. He was never tired of hearing stories about it: my own reminiscences as a small child, as a young woman, and as the wife of an officer in the famous 'Corps of Guides'.

When his own books began to do well he gave up working at David Higham's and became a full-time writer. And thereafter I was, technically, in David's charge. But in fact I continued to be advised by Paul, who would ring up or write at intervals to ask how I was getting on, and invite me to lunch to discuss whatever I was working on, plus life in general.

When my work on *The Far Pavilions* was interrupted by a nasty form of cancer, he would come and visit me in hospital, and I frequently had to implore him not to make me laugh, because it hurt like hell to do so. His visits were always enormously entertaining, for he would throw out ideas for new books – his, not mine – and discuss them with me. One, that I regret he never used, was tentatively entitled *The Leopards' House* and was to be about 'two people turning up from nowhere in some unusual place'. He would enlarge upon this for hours, until the bell rang for all visitors to leave, and it fascinated me. It still does. But that particular book was never written, though fragments of it appear, tantalizingly, in *The Corrida at San Feliu*.

Paul used to apply to my husband, Goff, for help over military details, and in the copy he sent us of *The Jewel in the Crown* he wrote 'with grateful thanks for their help; and their encouragement of someone who knows India less intimately than they do; and in the hope that they will recognize, affectionately, in this book, *their* India too.'

Though I had written to thank him for each signed copy of the 'Raj' novels that he sent as soon as it was in print, I had never commented on the books themselves. One day he rang up to enquire, with some tartness, the reason for this: was it because I disliked them? I said no, it was because I hadn't read them. And went on to explain that I made it a rule, when in labour with a novel, never to read a book by any writer whose work I deeply admired, because it only had the effect of making me depressingly aware of the defects in my own work, and gave me a howling inferiority complex. For which reason I restricted my reading to light-weight stuff that I knew I could equal. Paul said that I'd paid him the nicest compliment he'd ever had. But it wasn't a compliment. It was a plain statement of fact.

Only when I had at long last finished the *Pavilions* did I start reading *The Jewel in the Crown*, and then its three successors, at one gulp. And when I'd finished them, all I could say was that I'd have given anything to have written them myself.

Paul did the 'reader's report' of *Pavilions* for Allen Lane, and it was so detailed that he said of it that it was 'almost as long as the book'. It was a marvellous report, and one that I read with enormous pride. It also contained a lot of criticism and advice – most of which I took. But when I met him in London to discuss the book, I was shocked to see how ill he looked. He was just off to Tulsa, Oklahoma, to take up the post of visiting Professor of 'Eng. Lit.' for the autumn semester at the Faculty of Letters of Tulsa University. I remember he said that he wasn't going to write any more books about India, and thought he would try his hand at writing plays instead – which was something he had wanted to do for a long time. We walked back together toward Golden Square, and parted on a corner pavement; I was going to a Club in St James's Square, and he to David Higham's. I asked him if he really meant that he would never write anything more about India, and when he said 'yes', and I wanted to know why, he said slowly: 'Because I've nothing left to say.' I never saw him again, and later it occurred to me that it was a fitting 'curtain line' for the author of that marvellous quartet and its small, bright pendant, *Staying On*.

I spoke to him again, but only on the phone. I used to ring through to his hospital room in America, where they were trying to get him fit enough to stand an operation, and he used to chat away as entertainingly as ever. I think he was very lonely at that time. When I first heard it was cancer, I rang to say 'Anything I can do, you can do better', and that if I could defeat it, he could. I really believed that. There are so many people who would appear to be expendable, and so few Paul Scotts. But perhaps he did indeed speak prophetically when he told me that he 'had nothing left to say'.

The Cast

RALPH ARLISS (Captain Samuels) is the great nephew of the actor George Arliss. His television appearances include *The Day Christ Died, Quatermass, Love for Lydia, She Fell Among Thieves, Shoestring* and *Airline*.

He has acted with, among others, the Birmingham Repertory Company, the Welsh Theatre Company and at the Open Space Theatre.

His films include *Silhouettes, The Last Valley* and *Who Dares Wins*.

PEGGY ASHCROFT (Barbie Batchelor) made her professional stage debut in 1926 and has since made countless distinguished appearances, particularly in Shakespeare. In 1930, she played Desdemona to Paul Robeson's *Othello*, and two years later appeared as Juliet in John Gielgud's production of *Romeo and Juliet*. At the Shakespeare Memorial Theatre in Stratford in 1950, she appeared as Beatrice in *Much Ado About Nothing* and Cordelia in *King Lear*, both opposite John Gielgud. In the 1953 season, she played Portia in *The Merchant of Venice*, and Cleopatra opposite Michael Redgrave's Antony.

In the 1950s she also had great success as Hedda Gabler, in *The Chalk Garden*, and as Rebecca West in *Rosmersholm*. When the Royal Shakespeare Company was established in 1961, Peggy Ashcroft became an Associate Artist and since then has made many memorable appearances with the RSC, where she is a member of the directorate. Among her outstanding roles are Margaret of Anjou in *The Wars of the Roses*, Mrs Alving in *Ghosts*, Agnes in Albee's *A Delicate Balance*, Beth in Pinter's *Landscape*, Katherine in *Henry VIII*, the wife in *All Over*, also by Albee, and Lidya in *Old World*.

She filmed her role as Barbie in *The Jewel in the Crown* while she was making her latest appearance with the RSC as the Countess in *All's Well That Ends Well*, which was included in the company's first season at its new theatre in the Barbican Centre. Outside the RSC, Peggy Ashcroft joined the National Theatre to appear in *John Gabriel Borkman*, as Winnie in *Happy Days* and in *Watch on the Rhine* and, in a rare West End appearance, starred opposite Ralph Richardson in *Lloyd George Knew My Father*.

On television she appeared with Harry Andrews in *The Last Journey*, and in Ibsen's *Little Eyolf*, when the cast also included Charles Dance. Her roles in Stephen Poliakoff's *Caught on a Train* and Dennis Potter's *Cream in My Coffee* won her a British Academy award in 1980 as best television actress.

Peggy Ashcroft, who was made a Dame in 1956, previously filmed in India when she appeared in the James Ivory film *Hullabaloo over George and Bonnie's Pictures*.

Ralph Arliss

Peggy Ashcroft

Geoffrey Beevers

Derrick Branche

James Bree

Anthony Brown

Jeremy Child

GEOFFREY BEEVERS (Captain Coley) trained at the London Academy of Music and Dramatic Art after reading history at Oxford University. He has appeared regularly in lunchtime theatre for the Richmond Fringe Theatre Group, including the title role in *Uncle Vanya*. In the West End he appeared in *A Bequest to the Nation* and *Dandy Dick*, while film credits include *Victor/Victoria*, *Ivanhoe* and *The Curse of the Pink Panther*.

His television roles include Lloyd George in *Edward VII*, *The Critic*, *The White Guard*, *The Brack Report* and *Father's Day*. He is an active broadcaster as both writer and performer.

DERRICK BRANCHE (Ahmed) has appeared in *The Borgias* and *Crown Court*, as well as *Into The Labyrinth* and *Only When I Laugh*. He appeared at the Royal Exchange Theatre, Manchester, in *The Ordeal of Gilbert Pinfold* and at the Coliseum for the English National Opera production of *Salome*.

JAMES BREE (Colonel Grace) was in India for two years at the end of the War. On his return he joined the Central School of Speech and Drama and made his debut in the West End in a production of *The Love of Four Colonels* as Peter Ustinov's understudy.

His many television productions during thirty-three years as an actor include *Secret Army*, *Tales of Beatrix Potter*, *Father's Day*, *In Loving Memory* (with Thora Hird) and *Love among the Artists* for Granada Television, when he worked with Geraldine James, playing the part of her uncle.

He appeared in the Royal Shakespeare Company's opening production at the Aldwych and later worked with Dame Peggy Ashcroft in *The Duchess of Malfi*, *The Taming of the Shrew* and *A Winter's Tale*. He recently appeared in *The Importance of Being Earnest* at The Old Vic.

ANTHONY BROWN (Rev Arthur Peplow) began a theatrical career after university and the Army, when his first job with the Royal Shakespeare Company lasted three years and took him on tour to Russia. He has also been a member of the National Theatre Company, where productions included *The Freeway* – with Rachel Kempson – *The Elephant Man* and *Measure for Measure*, and with whom he visited the Baltimore Theatre Festival with the double-bill of *The Browning Version* and *Harlequinade*.

Recent television includes *The Clarion Van*, *The Remainder Man*, *Reilly*, and the BBC Shakespeare series productions of *Henry VI* and *Richard III*. He played Sir Robert Peel in *Disraeli*, and appears in the Paul McCartney film *Give My Regards to Broad Street*.

JEREMY CHILD (Robin White) appears in the Paul McCartney film *Give My Regards to Broad Street*, while other films include *Chanel Solitaire*, *Oh What a Lovely War*, *Young Winston* and *The Breaking of Bumbo*.

On television he has been seen in *Wings*, *Edward and Mrs Simpson*, *Anna Karenina*, *Coronation Street*, *Days of Hope*, *Suez*, *Winston Churchill – The*

Wilderness Years and *Bergerac*. In the theatre he appeared in *Conduct Unbecoming, Donkey's Years* and *Robert and Elizabeth*.

WARREN CLARKE (Dixon) played Winston Churchill in the television series *Jennie* and Quasimodo in a dramatization of *The Hunchback of Notre Dame*. He was also seen in James Cameron's television play *To the Sound of the Guns, The Onedin Line, The Tempest* – in which he played Caliban – *The Jail Diary of Albie Sachs, The Home Front* and *Reilly*. He was in *The Battle of Waterloo*, the first live play in the season of productions from the Pebble Mill studios.

His stage appearances include *Home* with John Gielgud and Ralph Richardson, *The Changing Room, I Claudius* and, as a member of the National Theatre, *Tales from the Vienna Woods, Force of Habit, Volpone* and *Lark Rise*. Recent films include *From a Far Country, Enigma, Firefox* and *The Cold Room*.

Warren Clarke

ROWENA COOPER (Connie White) played Lady Elizabeth Grey, later Queen Elizabeth, in the recent BBC Shakespeare series productions of *Henry VI Part III* and *Richard III*. She also appeared in *The Home Front* and the television dramatization of Iris Murdoch's *The Bell*. She played Enid Blyton in Michael Frayn's play *Liberty Hall* at Greenwich, and as a National Theatre player appeared in *Blithe Spirit, Old Movies* and *Watch It Come Down*. With the Bristol Old Vic she played Blanche Dubois in *A Streetcar Named Desire* and Martha in *Who's Afraid of Virginia Woolf?*.

Rowena Cooper

ANNA CROPPER (Nicky Paynton) played the title role in the television play *Where Is Betty Buchus?* and the TV critic in the Playhouse production *Preview*. She has appeared as defence counsel in *Crown Court*, while her many other productions include *Country Matters, Old Times, Nanny, The Lost Boys* with Tim Pigott-Smith, and *Maybury*. John Bowen's *Robin Redbreast* was specially written for her.

She appeared in Jack Gold's film *Praying Mantis, All Neat in Black Stockings* and *Cromwell*. Her theatre work includes London productions of *Separate Tables, John Bull's Other Island* and *Little Boxes*.

Anna Cropper

CHARLES DANCE (Guy Perron) joined the Royal Shakespeare Company in 1975, and roles included Catesby in *Richard III*, Lancaster in *Henry IV Parts I and II,* Buckingham in *Henry VI Part II* and Tullus Aufidius in *Coriolanus*. He took over the title role of *Henry V* in an RSC tour to New York in 1975, and took over the role of Coriolanus on a tour to Paris in 1979.

Earlier repertory work included Robin Philips's production of *The Beggar's Opera* and Jonathan Miller's *The Taming of the Shrew*. On television, he played the Duke of Clarence in *Edward VII*, Siegfried Sassoon in *The Fatal Spring* and Borghejm in *Little Eyolf* with Peggy Ashcroft. He also appeared in *Frost in May, Nancy Astor* and

Charles Dance

121

Fabia Drake

Nicholas Farrell

Shreela Ghosh

Matyelok Gibbs

Carol Gillies

John Pilger's play *The Last Day*. He was in the James Bond film *For Your Eyes Only*.

FABIA DRAKE (Mabel Layton) the youngest-ever student at the Royal Academy of Dramatic Art when she attended at the age of nine. One of her first leading roles came in *The Happy Family* with Noël Coward. Among her fellow actors when she played juvenile leads were Tallulah Bankhead, C. Aubrey Smith and Dame Marie Tempest. Through her association with Dame Marie, she met W. Bridges Adams who brought her to Stratford-upon-Avon as his leading lady when his new theatre opened in 1932. In her early twenties she became that theatre's first Rosalind, Portia, Beatrice and Viola.

On her marriage to barrister Maxwell Turner in 1938 she unofficially 'retired' from acting, but after his death in 1960 she returned to her career. She has enjoyed a wide variety of work from appearing in a comedy sketch with Derek Nimmo to reading her own compilation of poetry on the Third Programme. She played Bertie Wooster's Aunt Agatha in *The World of Wooster* and Leslie Crowther's mother in *Big Boy Now*. She recently appeared in *Let There Be Love*.

NICHOLAS FARRELL (Teddie Bingham) played Aubrey Montague in *Chariots of Fire* and appears in *Greystokes* as Belcher. He appeared in John Wells's *Anyone For Denis?* at the Whitehall Theatre, and in the double bill of *Lone Star/Private Wars* at the Bush Theatre. Among roles at the Bristol Old Vic, he played Henry VIII in *A Man for All Seasons*. Television productions include *Maybury*, *The White Guard* and *The Manhood of Edward Robinson* in The Agatha Christie Hour series.

SHREELA GHOSH (Minnie) has appeared on television in *The Garland*, *The Prince and the Demons*, *Moving on the Edge* and *Angels*. In the theatre, she has been seen in *The Shadow Prince*, *Blind Edge* and *Doolaly Days*.

MATYELOK GIBBS (Sister Ludmila) has been involved for twenty-five years in all aspects of children's theatre, and was artistic director of the Unicorn Theatre from 1973 to 1977.

She has appeared at the Warehouse and on tour with the Royal Shakespeare Company, and was in Blake Edwards's *Victor/Victoria*. She also appears in the First Love film *Secrets*. She appeared in *The Workshop* at the Hampstead Theatre and in the later television version. Early in 1983 she appeared, again at Hampstead, in Martin Sherman's *Messiah* and in the subsequent transfer to the Aldwych Theatre.

CAROL GILLIES (Clarissa Peplow) has played both Lady Bracknell and Miss Prism in separate repertory productions of *The Importance of Being Earnest* among extensive theatre work. She was in the première production of *The Dresser* at the Royal Exchange Theatre, Manchester, and played Goneril in *King Lear* at the Old Vic.

She has directed, among other productions, the

musical version of *Canterbury Tales* – in which she has appeared in England – for the West Canada Theatre Company and *Swan Song* for the Century Theatre Company. She appeared in Mai Zetterling's film *Scrubbers* and on television in Jack Gold's film *Praying Mantis*, and *Widows*.

Carol Gillies is a Cambridge graduate with a degree in physics and a post-graduate certificate in philosophy of science.

RENNEE GODDARD (Dr Anna Klaus) lives in Munich where she does much of her work. She appeared in *The Diary of Bridget Hitler* and the documentary *The Aliens*. In the theatre she has appeared in English-speaking productions of *Hedda Gabler* and *The Good Woman of Setzuan*, and played Queen Victoria in a German radio programme.

Rennee Goddard

JONATHAN and NICHOLAS HALEY (Edward Bingham) appeared in the film *The Eye of the Needle*, with Donald Sutherland and Kate Nelligan, playing – as they do in *The Jewel in the Crown* – the same character. In the Royal Shakespeare Company's production of *A Doll's House* at the Pit in the Barbican they played different parts in two separate casts, though there were occasions when they appeared in the same performance.

The twins celebrated their seventh birthday in March 1983, and live in Surrey with their parents, elder brother Christopher and younger brother Alastair.

Jonathan and *Nicholas Haley*

PATRICIA HENEGHAN (Mrs Peabody) toured India in a production of *Twelfth Night* in 1959 when she played Viola, and followed this with an appearance as Lady Percy opposite Sean Connery in a television production of *Henry IV*. Her West End theatre roles include *The Plumber's Progress* and *Once a Catholic*, and she was in the Manchester Royal Exchange Theatre production of *Hope against Hope*. On television she has been seen in *Lady Killers*, *Prisoners of Conscience*, *The Bell* and *Maybury*.

Patricia Heneghan

JANET HENFREY (Edwina Crane) spent seven years with the Royal Shakespeare Company up to 1976 where her roles included Mistress Quickly in *The Merry Wives of Windsor* and Emilia in Trevor Nunn's production of *The Winter's Tale* with Judi Dench. She appeared in the West End run of Ronald Harwood's *The Dresser*, and played the title role in *Ella* at the ICA.

Her films include *Reds* and *The Tamarind Seed*, and television productions include *Martin Chuzzlewit*, *Silas Marner*, *A Tale of Two Cities*, *Stand Up*, *Nigel Barton*, *Churchill's People*, *Great Expectations* and *Jury*.

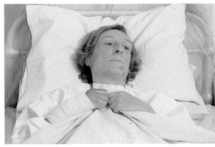

Janet Henfrey

BERNARD HORSFALL (Rankin) played Dr Martell in the television series *Enemy at the Door* and appears in the television film *Inside the Third Reich* for America's ABC Network. He played Sherlock Holmes for the Actors Company in *To Kill a King* and toured with Miriam Karlin in *Who's Afraid of*

Bernard Horsfall

John Horsley

Saeed Jaffrey

Geraldine James

Robert James

Virginia Woolf?. At the Palace Theatre, Watford, he appeared opposite Margaret Tyzack in Ira Levin's play *Veronica's Room* and, after working on *The Jewel in the Crown*, appeared as Prospero in *The Tempest* at St George's Theatre, London.

His film credits include *Guns at Batasi, On Her Majesty's Secret Service, Gold* and *Shout at the Devil*.

JOHN HORSLEY (Malcolm) has presided over more than thirty cases as Mr Justice Mowbray in *Crown Court*. His many comedy series include *The Fall and Rise of Reginald Perrin, Last of the Summer Wine, Leave It to Charlie* and *Hi De Hi*. He has appeared in more than 200 television plays and series, including *Upstairs Downstairs, Why Didn't They Ask Evans?, Clayhanger* and *Chessgame,* while numerous films include *Ben-Hur, Sink the Bismark* and *Terror on the Train*.

SAEED JAFFREY (Nawab) began an acting and broadcasting career in his native India in the 1950s before a Fulbright Scholarship took him to the United States where he obtained a second MA degree from the Catholic University of America in Washington.

He became the first Indian actor to gain a major Broadway role when he played opposite Dame Gladys Cooper in *A Passage to India*. After off-Broadway productions and a Brecht tour with Lotte Lenya, he moved to Britain where he appeared in the West End, and wrote and acted for the BBC World Service. In 1972 he played opposite Michael Redgrave in James Cameron's radio play *The Pump*. Television appearances include *Two's Company, Crown Court, Gangsters, Destiny* and *Minder*. He played Mr Bhoolabhoy in Granada's dramatization of Paul Scott's *Staying On* with Celia Johnson and Trevor Howard.

His films include *The Man Who Would Be King, Hullabaloo over George and Bonnie's Pictures* with Peggy Ashcroft, *The Guru* and *The Chess Players* with Richard Attenborough, for whom he played Sardar Patel, the prosperous lawyer who became Nehru's deputy, in the Oscar-winning film *Gandhi*.

GERALDINE JAMES (Sarah Layton) plays Mirabehn, daughter of an English admiral and dedicated follower of the Indian leader, in Richard Attenborough's Oscar-winning film *Gandhi*. She made a great impact in the title role of the television production of *Dummy*, and followed this with roles in *Love Among the Artists, The History Man* and *I Remember Nelson*, the last of which also featured Tim Pigott-Smith.

She appeared in the West End stage production of *The Passion of Dracula,* and as Vittoria Corombona in the Oxford Playhouse production of *The White Devil*. Before filming *Gandhi*, Geraldine's films included *Sweet William* and *Night Cruiser*.

ROBERT JAMES (Colonel Beames) read law at Glasgow University and then gained wide experience in repertory theatres in Scotland and England. His television productions include *The*

Onedin Line, Lives of Our Own, Northern Lights, Nanny, Frost in May and *Shackleton*. In the film *Mary Queen of Scots* he appeared as John Knox, and made a West End appearance in *After the Rain*. He appeared as George in an Edinburgh production of Tom Stoppard's *Jumpers*.

PETER JEFFREY (Mr Peabody) played Judge Brack in *Hedda Gabler* with Eileen Atkins in a Guildford production in 1982, and was in *The Faith Healer* in Santa Fe and San Francisco. In the West End he appeared in *Moving* and *Donkey's Years*, both with Penelope Keith, and at the National Theatre was in *For Services Rendered* and *When We Are Married*. At the RSC's London theatre, the Aldwych, he appeared in *Jingo*.

His most recent television credits include *Juliet Bravo, The Skeleton Key* in *Tales of the Unexpected, Nanny, Bognor, All's Well That Ends Well* and *Minder*. Film roles include *Britannia Hospital, Midnight Express, The Return of the Pink Panther* and *The Odessa File*.

Peter Jeffrey

KAMINI KAUSHAL (Aunt Shalini) began her film career in 1945 and has since worked in more than 100 films, first as a leading lady and now as a character actress. She has travelled extensively abroad as a member of Indian Government delegations and for film festivals. She wrote, directed and compèred a weekly children's programme on television in Bombay, where she now lives, and has been closely involved with the Indian Government's Children's Film Society. She has also written on children's cinema in magazine articles.

Kamini Kaushal

RACHEL KEMPSON (Lady Manners) is married to Sir Michael Redgrave and their children Vanessa, Lynn and Corin all followed their parents on to the professional stage. She met her husband when she joined the company of the Liverpool Playhouse for the 1934-5 season. The previous year, Rachel Kempson made her stage debut at Stratford's Memorial Theatre when, straight from the Royal Academy of Dramatic Art, she played Juliet and Ophelia, as well as Hero in *Much Ado About Nothing*, in a season when Stratford's leading lady was Fabia Drake.

Twenty years later she returned to Stratford, where her roles included Regan to the King Lear played by her husband, and Octavia to Peggy Ashcroft's Cleopatra. The next year the two actresses appeared together when Rachel Kempson played Mrs Elvsted to Peggy Ashcroft's Hedda Gabler. In 1956 she was a member of George Devine's company for the first season of the English Stage Company at the Royal Court, and she and Peggy Ashcroft both appeared in Brecht's *The Good Woman of Setzuan*. She made further appearances at Stratford and in the West End, and in 1974 joined the National Theatre Company to appear in Peter Nichols's *The Freeway*. She played opposite Alec Guinness in both *A Family and a Fortune* and *The Old Country*.

Television appearances include *Love for Lydia,*

Rachel Kempson

Rosemary Leach

David Leland

Nicholas le Prevost

Marne Maitland

Jude the Obscure, Jennie, and, more recently, *The Boxwallah* and the dramatization of Iris Murdoch's *The Bell.* She and her daughter Lynn appeared in the film *The Virgin Soldiers.*

ROSEMARY LEACH (Aunt Fenny) won the 1982 SWET award as best actress in a new play for her role as Helene Hanff in the London production of *84 Charing Cross Road.* Television appearances include *The Power Game, Life Begins at Forty,* her own series *Sadie It's Cold Outside* and *Roads to Freedom.* She played Queen Victoria in *Disraeli,* Annie Besant in *Warrior's Return,* and appeared in Laurence Olivier's production of *Hindle Wakes.* Her performance in the television dramatization of *Cider with Rosie* won her a nomination for the Best Actress of the Year award, and she has been nominated on four other occasions.

Recent television includes the BBC Shakespeare series production of *All's Well That Ends Well* and *Othello* – in which she played Emilia – and *The Critic.* Her films include the remake of *Brief Encounter, That'll Be the Day* and *SOS Titanic.* Her theatre work includes *Just Between Ourselves, Travelling North, The Beggar's Opera* and the Royal Court production of *Other Worlds.*

DAVID LELAND (Purvis) appears in the films *The Missionary* and *Time Bandits,* and the television series *Ripping Yarns* and *The Hitch-hiker's Guide to the Galaxy.* He appeared in the ITV play *Miss Morrison's Ghosts* and the 'Play of the Month' production of Solzhenitsyn's *The Love Girl and the Innocent.*

As a theatre director he has been responsible for staging the work of many of today's new dramatists, including *Talent* by Victoria Wood and *Says I Says He* by Ron Hutchins, many of which were first put on during his period as a director at Sheffield's Crucible Theatre.

Earlier this year four controversial films on the British education system for which he wrote the screenplays – *Birth of a Nation, Flying into the Wind, Rhino* and *Made in Britain* – were screened on ITV.

He is also the author of two 'Play for Today' dramas – *Psy-Warriors* first produced in the theatre, and *Beloved Enemy.*

NICHOLAS LE PREVOST (Rowan) appeared in both *Brideshead Revisited* – as the doctor attending Sebastian in North Africa – and *The Borgias.* He was one of the resident ghosts in the children's drama series *The Ghosts of Motley Hall,* and has also appeared in *Penmarric, Strangers, Shelley* and *The Imitation Game.* He appeared with Kika Markham in the two-character television play *What About Borneo?* by Tom Kempinski. He spent a season with the Royal Shakespeare Company at the Warehouse Theatre, and appeared in *Dracula* at the Young Vic.

MARNE MAITLAND (Pandit Baba) has been based in Rome since 1972 from where his film roles have taken him throughout Europe and Asia. He appears in Peter Ustinov's film *Memed* and counts among his earlier screen appearances *Anne of a*

126

Thousand Days, Jesus of Nazareth, Ashanti and *The Trail of the Pink Panther*. He has also appeared in such epic productions as *Bhowani Junction, Nine Hours to Rama* and *Khartoum*.

Art Malik

ART MALIK (Hari Kumar) trained at the Guildhall School of Music and Drama, and among his repertory work were productions of *Comedians, Destiny* and *Whose Life Is It Anyway?*. He appeared in a short season with the RSC in London and, with the Prospect Theatre Company, he appeared at the Old Vic in *Romeo and Juliet, The Government Inspector* and *The 88*. On television he has been seen in *Mixed Blessings, Crown Court, Bergerac* and the film *Richard's Things*. His films include Peter Brook's *Meetings with Remarkable Men,* and he appears in the dramatization of *The Far Pavilions*.

ZIA MOHYEDDIN (MAK) made his London stage debut in 1960 in *A Passage to India*, a part he repeated in his first New York appearance two years later. He spent most of the 1970s in Pakistan as Director-General of the country's National Performing Ensemble.

Zia Mohyeddin

His film debut was in *Lawrence of Arabia*, and subsequent films include *Sammy Going South, Khartoum* and *Ashanti*. His numerous television appearances include *Gangsters, Death of a Princess,* and Granada's *Staying On*. He is presenter and producer of Central Television's *Here and Now,* and also appeared in the live production of Fay Weldon's *Redundant! Or the Wife's Revenge*, which starred Judy Parfitt.

WENDY MORGAN (Susan Layton) won the *Evening Standard's* Most Promising New Actress award for her role as Mollie in John Schlesinger's *Yanks*, and received critical praise for her part as Ruby in the television series *Pictures*. She played Bianca in Jonathan Miller's television production of *Othello,* and other television productions include *Soldiers Talking Cleanly, Sheppey, Dick Turpin, New Girl in Town* and *Across the Water*. Film appearances include *The Mirror Crack'd*, and *The Birth of the Beatles* in which she played Cynthia Lennon.

Wendy Morgan

She played the title role in the Manchester Royal Exchange Theatre production of *Cinderella* and, since completing work on *The Jewel in the Crown*, has appeared as Babe in the British première of Beth Henley's Broadway success *Crimes of the Heart* at the Bush Theatre.

ALBERT MOSES (Suleiman) appears in the latest James Bond film *Octopussy* and the film *Scandalous*. He was also seen in *An American Werewolf in London* and *Pink Floyd – The Wall*.

Albert Moses

At the National Theatre he was in the cast of *The Freeway* and *Phaedra Britannica*, and on television his many varied productions include *Mind Your Language, The Rag Trade, Staying On* and *The Chinese Detective*.

JUDY PARFITT (Mildred Layton) played Cleopatra to Keith Baxter's Antony in a Young Vic production of Shakespeare's play after completing her filming on *The Jewel in the Crown*. She also

Judy Parfitt

Salmaan Peer

Tim Pigott-Smith

Eric Porter

appeared in *Redundant! Or the Wife's Revenge*, the second of a series of plays transmitted live from BBC's Pebble Mill studios. She co-starred with Prunella Scales in the television play *Grand Duo*, and appeared as Roger Ackerley's mistress Muriel in *Secret Orchards*. Other notable television roles came in *Northern Lights, The Breadwinner, Malice Aforethought* and *The Family Dance* in which she had also appeared on stage.

At the Royal Court Theatre, she was seen in D. H. Lawrence's *The Daughter-in-Law* and *The Widowing of Mrs Holroyd*, as well as *The Hotel in Amsterdam* and *The Duchess of Malfi*. She played Gertrude in Tony Richardson's production of *Hamlet*, and was in Peter Gill's production of *The Cherry Orchard* at the Riverside Studios.

SALMAAN PEER (Sayed Kasim) wrote and directed the drama documentary film *Maila*, premiered at the 1983 Edinburgh Film Festival and scheduled for a later screening on Channel 4. His latest film enterprise is *Wild Roses*, a drama dealing with a tribal feud on India's North West Frontier. Salmaan Peer is the son of a famous Indian playwright, and began work in the Indian film industry. He settled in Britain in 1963 and has made many television and film appearances since then. He spent a year in *Emergency Ward 10*, and his feature films include *Private Enterprise, The Twisted Nerve* and *The Blood Of Hussain*. He appears in the *All For Love* film *Mrs Silly* with Maggie Smith.

TIM PIGOTT-SMITH (Ronald Merrick) graduated in drama from Bristol University and joined the city's Old Vic Company after training at their theatre school. He has been a member of Prospect Theatre Company and the RSC, and with the latter spent most of one year commuting between Stratford – where he played Posthumus in *Cymbeline* – and the Aldwych Theatre – where he was Dr Watson in *Sherlock Holmes*. He later appeared in the Broadway run of *Sherlock Holmes*. He played Angelo in *Measure for Measure* and Hotspur in *Henry IV Part I* in the BBC production of the Shakespeare canon, while other prominent television appearances include *The Lost Boys, Winston Churchill – The Wilderness Years, Fame Is the Spur*, and *I Remember Nelson*, in which he played Captain Hardy.

His films include *Aces High, Joseph Andrews, Clash of the Titans, Escape to Victory*, the new version of *The Hunchback of Notre Dame* and *The Day Christ Died*.

ERIC PORTER (Count Bronowsky) made his stage debut when he walked on in the 1945 Shakespeare Memorial Theatre Company's production of *Twelfth Night*. Fifteen years later he played Malvolio with the same company, then newly re-named the Royal Shakespeare Company at the start of a long association with them. His many leading roles with the RSC include the title roles in *Becket* and *Macbeth*, Pope Pius XII in *The Representative,* and *Henry IV*. In 1965 he doubled the role of Shylock in *The Merchant of Venice* with

Barabas in Marlowe's *The Jew of Malta*. In 1968 he played the title roles in *Dr Faustus* and *King Lear,* the latter of which, with Uncle Vanya, he describes as his favourite part. He played Mr Darling and Captain Hook in the 1971 Christmas staging of *Peter Pan.*

Eric Porter enjoyed a huge success as Soames Forsyte in the television dramatization of *The Forsyte Saga.* He played Karenin in a television version of *Anna Karenina,* and Polonius in the BBC Shakespeare series production of *Hamlet.* He appeared as General Alanbrooke in *Churchill and the Generals,* and as Neville Chamberlain in *Churchill – The Wilderness Years.* He won the *Evening Standard* Award as Best Actor of 1959 for his role as Rosmer in Ibsen's *Rosmersholm* opposite Peggy Ashcroft.

Om Puri

OM PURI (De Souza) is one of India's best-known film actors and is based in Bombay. He trained at the National Theatre School in Delhi, and has worked extensively with such noted directors as Satyajit Ray and Shyam Benegal. His films include *Aakrosh,* for which he won a best actor award in 1982, and *Kal Yug.* He plays the role of Nahari in Richard Attenborough's film *Gandhi.*

Norman Rutherford

NORMAN RUTHERFORD (Mr Maybrick) resumed an acting career in his retirement, after twenty years as a senior drama executive with BBC Television, and celebrated his seventieth birthday while filming his role in *The Jewel in the Crown.* He made his professional stage debut in Bournemouth in 1936. Since returning to acting his productions have included *Anna Karenina, Poldark, Wuthering Heights, Henry IV Part I* and *Prince Regent.*

As a National Theatre player for three years until 1982, he appeared in many productions, including *Galileo, Man and Superman, Amadeus,* and *The Oresteia.* He performed in the latter when the drama was staged in the Greek auditorium where it was first produced.

Dev Sagoo

DEV SAGOO (Vidyasagar) trained at the Birmingham Theatre School, and has had leading roles in the television plays *A Touch of Eastern Promise* and *Baby Love.* He appeared in the television version of the RSC's musical staging of *The Comedy of Errors* and is a regular presenter of the children's programme *Playschool.*

He was in the cast of Horace Ove's play *The Garland.*

Zohra Segal

ZOHRA SEGAL (Lili Chatterjee) was a leading actress and dance director with Prithvi Theatres, Bombay, from 1945 to 1959, and toured extensively throughout India during this period. For the next three years she was the principal of the NATYA Academy for Dance and Drama, New Delhi. Her television work in Britain since 1963 includes *Kipling, The Expert, Dr Who, Neighbours* and *Mind Your Language.*

She has appeared in films which include *The Long Duel, The Guru* and *Quest for Fire,* while in the theatre she played a leading role in *The Primary*

Frederick Treves

Stuart Wilson

Susan Wooldridge

English Class at the Orange Tree, Richmond, and its transfer to the West End.

FREDERICK TREVES (Colonel Layton) appeared in the screen version of *The Elephant Man*, a film in which his great-uncle the famous surgeon Sir Frederick Treves – who treated the Victorian freak – was also portrayed. He has recently been a member of the National Theatre Company, with whom he appeared in *The Iceman Cometh, Much Ado About Nothing, Caritas* and *Don Juan*. Earlier he appeared with them in David Hare's *Plenty* and *The Philanderer*. He appeared in television productions of *The Cherry Orchard* and Trevor Griffiths's *Country*, and was also in *PQ 17*. He also appears in *A Flame to the Phoenix*, and the dramatization of C. P. Snow's *Strangers and Brothers*. He played the colonel-in-chief in the television series *The Regiment*, and has also appeared in *Warship, The Sinking of HMS Victoria*, and *Destiny*.

STUART WILSON (Major Clark) has played in several Royal Shakespeare Company productions including *Henry IV Part I*, as Hotspur, directed by Terry Hands, and Laertes in *Hamlet*, directed by Buzz Goodbody. He has also played Worthy in the Cambridge Theatre Company production of *The Recruiting Officer*. His television credits include, for the BBC, *The Old Men at the Zoo*, Vronsky in *Anna Karenina*, Ferdinand Lopez in *The Pallisers*, *I Claudius*. He also played Johann Strauss in *The Strauss Family*.

His films include *Ivanhoe* and *The Prisoner of Zenda* as Rupert of Hentzau.

SUSAN WOOLDRIDGE (Daphne Manners) followed her mother, the actress Margaretta Scott, into an acting career and as well as studying at the Central School of Speech and Drama, trained in Paris with Jacques Lecoq and with the Commedia del' Arte group in both London and Paris. Her extensive work in regional repertory theatre was recalled when she came to play the part of assistant stage manager Flick Harold in the comedy series *Rep*. Among her roles were Lady Teazle in *The School for Scandal*, and Lady Macbeth, and she played Alison in a Young Vic production of *Look Back in Anger*, directed by Mel Smith.

She also spent a season with the Common Stock Theatre Company. Her television productions include *Heydays Hotel, The Naked Civil Servant, Lady Killers, Napoleon and Love,* and *Emmerdale Farm*. She has appeared in two films starring Alan Bates – *The Shout* directed by Jerzy Skolimowski, and *Butley* directed by Harold Pinter.

The Production team

CHRISTOPHER MORAHAN, producer and co-director of *The Jewel in the Crown*, has worked extensively in television and the theatre.

In the Granada season of National Theatre plays in 1980 he directed Alan Ayckbourn's *Bedroom Farce*. Stage productions at the National Theatre – where he was an associate director from 1977 to 1981, and deputy to Peter Hall from 1978 to 1981 – include *State Of Revolution, The Philanderer, Brand, The Wild Duck, Strife, Sisterly Feelings*, and *Man and Superman*.

Christopher Morahan was Head of Plays at the BBC from 1972 to 1976. His productions for television include Pinter's *Old Times*, Peter Nichols's *Hearts and Flowers, The Gorge* and *The Common, Uncle Vanya*, the John Hopkins quartet *Talking to a Stranger,* and *John Gabriel Borkman* with Laurence Olivier.

His association with Granada began with a production of *Giants and Ogres*, by Alun Owen, in 1971, and since then, among other plays, he has directed for Granada *Some Distant Shadow* by John Hopkins and *Three Months Gone* by Donald Howarth.

He has twice won the Society of Film and Television Arts award, for *Emergency Ward 10* and *The Letter*.

Other theatre work includes Jules Feiffer's *Little Murders* for the Royal Shakespeare Company, John Hopkins's *This Story of Yours*, David Mercer's *Flint* and Pinter's *The Caretaker*.

JIM O'BRIEN, co-director of *The Jewel in the Crown*, was the director of *Another Day* in the BBC's 'Play of the Week' series, *Shadows on our Skin*, the much-acclaimed Play for Today about a young boy growing up in Londonderry, and *Jake's End,* a BBC Playhouse production.

He has directed a number of documentaries and fiction films, including an adaptation of a Doris Lessing short story which was shown at various international film festivals in 1976 and 1977, and a BBC-2 Open Door, *Black Future*, a film made with unemployed West Indians, which was also shown at festivals in London and the USA.

Between 1968 and 1973 Jim O'Brien worked mainly in the subsidized theatre and his appointments included Associate Director of Newcastle's Tyneside Theatre Company and Artistic Director of the Soho Poly for 1973.

Jim O'Brien was a student at the National Film School, and subsequently returned to supervise workshops.

KEN TAYLOR, who has adapted 'The Raj Quartet' for television, was born near Bolton, Lancashire. He joined the RAF as a wireless operator and was posted to India in 1941. He entered the Old Vic Theatre School on a technical production course, and was the founder director of Leatherhead Repertory Theatre.

Ken Taylor has been a full-time writer since 1956. His first work for Granada was the adaptation of D. H. Lawrence's *The Widowing Of Mrs Holroyd*, which was followed by adaptations of Lawrence's *The Blind Man, In Love* and *The Prussian Officer*.

In 1964 he received the Writer of the Year award for his television trilogy *The Seekers*, and in the same year his ATV play *The Devil and John Brown* won the Writers' Guild award for the best original television play.

His many other television dramatizations have included Muriel Spark's *The Girls of Slender Means*, Rebecca West's *The Birds Fall Down*, Thomas Hardy's *The Melancholy Hussar* in the series *Wessex Tales*, and Jane Austen's *Mansfield Park*.

In the Granada series *Shades of Darkness* seen in the summer of 1983, he has adapted *The Lady's Maid's Bell* by Edith Wharton, *Seaton's Aunt* by Walter de la Mare, and *The Maze* by C. H. B. Kitchin.

IRENE SHUBIK (series originator) produced the Granada dramatization of Paul Scott's *Staying On* with Celia Johnson and Trevor Howard. She originated and produced the first series of *Rumpole of the Bailey*, having first produced it as a single play in the 'Play for Today' series at the BBC.

Other series produced at the BBC include *The Mind Beyond, Wessex Tales, Thirteen Against Fate* and *Out of the Unknown*. As producer of the 'Wednesday Play' and 'Play for Today' she was responsible for, among others, *Edna the Inebriate Woman*, with Patricia Hayes, *The Right Prospectus* by John Osborne and Peter Nichols's *Hearts and Flowers*.

Irene Shubik wrote and directed the film *Scrolls from the Son of a Star*, seen in the 'Chronicle' series.

MILLY PREECE (associate producer) joined Granada in 1966 as a secretary, becoming a production assistant in 1968. Her work during thirteen years as a production assistant includes the Laurence Olivier plays, the documentary series *The Christians* and the Ken Russell dramas *Clouds of Glory*. She became an associate producer in 1980 and worked on *My Father's House*.

VIC SYMONDS (production designer) designed the controversial feature film *The Long Good Friday*.

For Granada, he designed *Bedroom Farce*, directed by Christopher Morahan, *Lady Killers, The Zoo* and Trevor Griffiths's *Occupations*. His wide experience in television includes *Old Times, Electra, The Racing Game, The Main Chance, The Pump* and *The Power Game*.

ALAN PICKFORD (production designer) designed the West End theatre production of Alan Ayckbourn's *The Norman Conquests*, and more recently the Young Vic's staging of Kit Williams's

Masquerade. Other theatre work includes *My Fat Friend, Journey's End* and *The Winter's Tale.*

His television credits include the major series *The Brontës, Dickens of London* and *The Good Companions,* as well as episodes of *Tales of the Unexpected* and *Atom Spies.*

RAY GOODE (lighting cameraman) was singled out for his outstanding contribution to the success of *Brideshead Revisited.* While he was in India on *The Jewel in the Crown,* he heard that he had been elected to membership of the British Society of Cinematographers.

He joined Granada in 1961 as a rostrum cameraman, and his many productions as a lighting cameraman include *Gossip from the Forest, Hard Times, Another Sunday and Sweet FA, The Christians, Childhood,* nine episodes of *Country Matters,* including *The Mill* and *Breeze Anstey,* and Granada's pioneering drama-on-film *The Mosedale Horseshoe* – many of which have won international festival awards.

GEORGE FENTON (music composer) was responsible with Ravi Shankar for the score of Richard Attenborough's film *Gandhi.* He also wrote the signature tune for the BBC's early morning programme *Breakfast Time.*

Other television programmes for which he has composed music include *Bergerac, Going Gently, Camera, The History Man, Fox, Newsnight, Shoestring* and *Bill Brand.*

In the theatre, he has worked extensively at the National Theatre and for the Royal Shakespeare Company, where productions included *Twelfth Night, A Month in the Country, Don Juan, Much Ado About Nothing, Good* and *Macbeth.* Other film scores include *Hussy, Parole* and *Dead End.*

EDDIE MANSELL (film editor) worked with Leslie Woodhead on his major drama-documentary programmes *Invasion* and *Strike.* In addition to documentary work he also edited the filmed play *The Good Soldier,* directed by Kevin Billington. He previously worked as an editor on *World in Action.*

DIANE HOLMES (costume designer) began her work in the theatre after training at Kingston Polytechnic Fashion School, and after working as a private fashion consultant she joined the BBC for a number of drama series. Later she worked on the television dramatization of J. B. Priestley's *The Good Companions.*

For Granada, she designed the Victoria Wood play *Happy Since I Met You,* various light entertainment shows, and the children's drama series, *Dear Enemy.* She is hoping to move into the video world with her own cassette on needlework and design.

ESTHER DEAN (costume designer) won the first-ever award for costume design from the British Academy of Film and Television Arts for her work on the television dramatization of Dickens's *Hard Times.* Her many other productions at Granada include *Persuasion, Country Matters, The Ghosts of Motley Hall, Victorian Scandals* – in one of which Twiggy had her first dramatic role – *Cribb, Staying On* and *A Flame to the Phoenix.*

She is costume designer on the Granada production of *The Adventures of Sherlock Holmes,* the major dramatization of thirteen Conan Doyle stories.

BILL SHEPHARD joined Granada as a stagehand in 1973, and as a floor manager worked on *Hard Times, Clouds of Glory* and *Power Struggle.* His work as a Granada production manager includes *Strangers, House of Caradus, Print-Out, Fallen Hero, Closing Ranks, The Spoils of War* and *Lives of Our Own.* He began work on *The Jewel in the Crown* in the autumn of 1980.

IAN SCAIFE joined Granada as a graphics artist from ITN in 1973. He became a production manager in 1979 since when his work has included *The Spoils of War, Strangers, Cribb* and *A Kind of Loving.* He joined *The Jewel in the Crown* production team early in 1981.

SUSIE BRUFFIN (casting director) joined Granada in 1973 as a secretary in the company's casting department in London. She moved to the Manchester TV Centre four years later and among productions on which she worked was Ken Russell's *Clouds of Glory.* She became a casting director in 1978 and has worked on *Coronation Street, Crown Court* and *A Kind of Loving.* Her plays include *Print Out, The Zoo* and the Granada dramatisation of Paul Scott's *Staying On.*

JON WOODS (camera operator) studied geology at Hull University before starting his professional career as a sound assistant on an Open University programme. As a freelance camera assistant, he worked for the BBC in Cardiff, London and Scotland, and for Granada worked on *The Land of Ice-cream* and *Sam.*

He joined Granada in 1978 and worked with Ray Goode on *Man and Boy.* His many credits for the company include *Love Among the Artists, Cribb, A Kind of Loving, Strangers* and *Happy Since I Met You,* and – outside the drama field – *Union World* and *World in Action.*

MARTIN KAY (sound recordist) joined Granada Television in 1973 as a studio sound engineer, and moved to work on film sound in 1976. After some time with Granada's *World in Action* teams, he worked on drama series including *My Father's House* and *Aspects of Love.* He was on the production team of Granada's documentary series, *The Christians,* and worked in Afghanistan on the award-winning Granada report *Afghanistan Exodus.*

Producer/Director CHRISTOPHER MORAHAN
Director JIM O'BRIEN
Script KEN TAYLOR
Series Originator IRENE SHUBIK
Associate Producer MILLY PREECE
Production Designers VIC SYMONDS
        ALAN PICKFORD
Lighting Cameraman RAY GOODE
Music GEORGE FENTON
Film Editor EDWARD MANSELL
Costume Designers DIANE HOLMES
        ESTHER DEAN
Make-up Supervisor ANNA JONES
Production Managers BILL SHEPHARD
        IAN SCAIFE
Indian Location Consultants NIGAAR FILM WORKSHOP
        VALMIK THAPAR
        TEJBIR SINGH
Unit Manager LES DAVIS
Floor Manager JOHN NEWMAN
Production Assistants SUE WILD
        CHRISTINE WATT
Production Secretary ANNE DOUGHERTY
Production Office Secretary JANE HOUSTON
Assistant Stage Manager GORDON PLEASANT
Casting Directors SUSIE BRUFFIN
        PRISCILLA JOHN
Booking Assistant JUNE WEST
Designer NICK KING
Design Assistants CARLOTTA BARROW
        NEIL CALDWELL
Design Manager BILL TOMLINSON
Property Buyers ALAN RUTTER
        DAVID LIVSEY
Camera Operator JON WOODS
Camera Assistant LAWRENCE JONES
Clapper Loaders ALAN FRASER
        HOWARD SOMERS
Sound Recordists MARTIN KAY
        HARRY BROOKES
Sound Assistant TONY COOPER
Chief Grips KEN ROBERTS
Grips Assistant BOB GREGORY
Editing Assistants PETER DODD
        MARK SENIOR
Dubbing Editors CHRIS ACKLAND
        RICHARD DUNFORD
Dubbing Mixers JOHN WHITWORTH
        ANDY WYATT
Wardrobe Supervisor NOREEN INGHAM
Wardrobe JANET JOHNSON
        JOHN HUGHES
        PAUL WATTS
Make-up SALLIE ADAMS
        JANE HATCH
        LINDA PARKIN
        RUTH QUINN
Graphics JOHN LEECH
Researcher LESLEY BEAMES
Indian Advisor BHASKAR BHATTACHARYYA

Advisor on Military Costumes JOHN MOLLO
Indian Army Advisor COL. (retd) DENNIS REYNOLDS
Scene Masters PETER AVERY
        JOE EXTON
Assistant Scene Master BILL ROBERTS
Action Prop Man PETER MORAN
Prop Dressers DENNIS BLYTH
        JIM COYLE
        DAVE DAMPIER
        JOHN ECCLES
Stagehands BARRY EVITT
        MIKE KEHOE
        RUSS LEE
        TREVOR SCOTT
        BILLY WOODWORTH
Property Storeman CHRIS WALL
Carpenters DAVID CRANSHAW
        BOB CRICHTON
        BRIAN LAW
        PETER SKARRATT
        IAN SIMPSON
Painters RAY FROGGART
        PAUL HARRIS
        ARTHUR ORWIN
        LES WORRALL
Painters' Labourers ERIC ANDERSON
        LEN HARGREAVES
Foreman Electricians KEN GRAVILLE
        ALAN LONGSHAW
Chargehand Electricians BOB ACTON
        JIM CAMP
        PAUL ROONEY
        DAVE RATCLIFFE
        CHARLIE SHOREMAN
        DAVE SMYTH
Generator Operators STEVE HARDMAN
        KEITH JONES
        IAN JACKSON
        KEN PITTS
Cost Clerk WALTER LIVESEY
Photographers STEWART DARBY
        DAVID BURROWS
Press Officer PETER MARES

Picture Research: DIANA KORCHIEN